ONE SEASON IN ROCKET CITY

ONE SEASON

IN ROCKET CITY

How the 1985 Huntsville Stars Brought
Minor League Baseball Fever to Alabama

DALE TAFOYA

Foreword by Sandy Alderson

UNIVERSITY OF NEBRASKA PRESS | LINCOLN

The University of Nebraska Press is part of a land-grant institution with campuses and programs on the past, present, and future homelands of the Pawnee, Ponca, Otoe-Missouria, Omaha, Dakota, Lakota, Kaw, Cheyenne, and Arapaho Peoples, as well as those of the relocated Ho-Chunk, Sac and Fox, and Iowa Peoples.

Library of Congress Cataloging-in-Publication Data
Names: Tafoya, Dale, author.
Title: One season in Rocket City: how the 1985 Huntsville Stars brought minor league baseball fever to Alabama / Dale Tafoya; foreword by Sandy Alderson.
Description: Lincoln: University of Nebraska Press, [2023] | Includes bibliographical references and index.
Identifiers: LCCN 2022026636
ISBN 9781496230737 (hardback)
ISBN 9781496235688 (epub)
ISBN 9781496235695 (pdf)
Subjects: LCSH: Huntsville Stars (Baseball team) | Minor league baseball—Alabama—Huntsville—History. | Huntsville (Ala.)—Social life and customs. | BISAC: SPORTS & RECREATION / Baseball / History
Classification: LCC GV875.H86 T34 2023 | DDC 796.357/640761—dc23/eng/20220714
LC record available at https://lccn.loc.gov/2022026636

Set in Freight Text by Mikala R. Kolander.

"This is the most exciting thing that has happened to Huntsville since man landed on the moon."—**JOHN GLENN**, former Huntsville councilman, April 19, 1985

Contents

Foreword

SANDY ALDERSON

The inaugural season for the Huntsville Stars was special on so many levels. Nineteen-eighty-five marked professional baseball's return to Huntsville and many of the Oakland A's top prospects assembled there for a magical, championship season. As vice president of baseball operations for the A's, I was excited about our new partnership with Larry Schmittou's franchise and the city of Huntsville for hosting our Double-A club. But what happened there that season sure exceeded my expectations. The timing was perfect for the city and the rise of our prospects. Huntsville welcomed us with open arms, and we brought them some thrills. The city financed a sparkling new stadium for us, and we rewarded them with a star-studded roster that grew up together in our farm system. This resilient group of players, quality individuals, were conditioned to win.

To compliment the club, we sent them Brad Fischer, one of our most successful Minor League managers. He had fostered a winning culture with our Single-A farm club in Madison, Wisconsin, and we thought he was the right man for the job in Huntsville.

What made the team so special wasn't just the can't-miss prospects or the manager. The hungry players who never reached the Major Leagues proved to be the heart and soul of the club.

While we were rebuilding at the big league level in Oakland, we understood that the core of our future championship team was playing at Double-A Huntsville in 1985. The players we drafted in the early part of the decade—under scouting director Dick Wiencek—were showing promise and climbing our system. Some of our top prospects also came from trades. When we traded Rickey Henderson to the New York Yankees in December 1984, we acquired outfielder Stan Javier and pitcher Eric Plunk in the seven-player deal. Both players were crucial to Huntsville's success that season.

We also felt we had some of baseball's most innovative minds leading our farm system and helping shape the Huntsville roster. Karl Kuehl came over in 1983 to become the A's director of player development and put together a group of distinguished roving Minor League instructors to pass through our affiliates.

It was a time of transition for our organization. Coming off some magical years under Billy Martin, we needed to develop our own identity as a front office. Billy, you see, was the face of the A's. The new emphasis was developing players through our farm system. We couldn't afford to sign a superstar free agent at the time and recognized that focusing on the farm system was the way to go. The 1985 Huntsville Stars were the poster boys of the movement.

As Dale Tafoya captures in the book, the Stars made Huntsville smile in 1985 and left a lasting impression on many kids growing up in the area. The fascinating story is not only about what the club did on the diamond but how the community embraced the team and its individual players. Joe Davis Stadium became Huntsville's new popular venue. The city's enthusiasm for the club was a model for other cities and franchises. Dale chronicles in detail the circumstances that brought the club to Huntsville and describes the ups and downs of the season.

Surprisingly, as many top prospects were highlighted in the club, underdogs like Rocky Coyle and Pete Kendrick shined when it counted and brought Huntsville a championship. The Double-A classification of Minor League Baseball can make or break a prospect and playing in the sweltering conditions of the Southern League can be draining. The players battled through the competition that season and some of them later carried the Oakland A's to three straight World Series appearances from 1988 to 1990, including a championship in 1989. Some of them had long baseball careers elsewhere. Others became successful in non-baseball industries. The year 1985 was a fun one for popular culture and especially for Huntsville. I was thrilled to be associated with the incredible ride and season in Huntsville.

"Oakland is going to be a team to watch the next couple of years. That Huntsville team is one of the best Double-A clubs I've seen in a few years."
—**GEORGE DIGBY**, scout, Boston Red Sox, 1985

August 23, 1984: Joe W. Davis, Huntsville's mayor since 1968, finally pulled it off. By virtue of a 4–1 vote that Thursday night—in dramatic, late-inning fashion—the city council essentially approved Davis's dream for the city. In a packed council chamber, the members agreed on terms to bring professional baseball to Huntsville beginning with the 1985 season and build a new stadium to accommodate it. The city was starving for recreation and entertainment. It needed an attraction to bring the community together.

Davis felt having a team for the city to root for would fill the void and benefit the community in other ways. Once the vote was announced, cheering erupted in the chamber. For good reason. Davis's stubborn push to land a franchise almost never happened. The dizzying process was taxing for the sixty-five-year-old mayor of five terms. Almost two weeks before, on August 9, the prospects of a club coming to Huntsville looked bleak. The anxiety from the rollercoaster sessions caused Davis to pace around the lobby and smoke cigarettes during breaks. He had just come off winning a controversial mayoral election that barely avoided a July 31 runoff. The snag of the negotiations that kept the council from approving the eight-page proposal was authorizing beer sales in the heart of the Bible Belt. It wasn't Davis's idea.

Larry Schmittou, who owned the Double-A franchise Davis was trying to bring, insisted on selling beer in the proposed stadium or the deal was off. Backed by country music money, the forty-four-year-old Schmittou, vice president and director of marketing for the Texas Rangers, was growing an empire of Minor League clubs. Since 1978, he was one of baseball's top Minor League executives and marketing minds. He owned the Nashville Sounds, one of Minor League Baseball's most profitable franchises that played in the Southern League. He owned a franchise at every classification of the Minor Leagues. Schmittou had a golden touch. He was licensed to sell beer at Herschel Greer Stadium in Nashville, where the Sounds played. But even Schmittou's winning reputation couldn't sway the conservative council. They voted 5–0 against serving alcohol. Schmittou wouldn't budge on his demand to sell beer and the talks of bringing a franchise to Huntsville were dissolving. "I guess it's over," a disappointed Davis said after the vote.

Three days later, on August 12, a wild bench-clearing brawl between the Atlanta Braves and San Diego Padres at Atlanta-Fulton County Stadium didn't help the optics of selling alcohol in baseball stadiums. During the highly publicized fiasco, some fans showered players with beer from behind the dugout. Five fans were arrested, and seventeen players were ejected from the game. But Davis refused to let the negotiations die. He mustered support from key councilmembers and came up with the idea of a section designated for nondrinkers in the new ballpark. Schmittou and the council approved the compromise, and the city landed a pro club for the first time in fifty-five years. Huntsville became a new Southern League entry. "We do have a ball club," a relieved Davis said.

Despite the optimism, there was uncertainty about the interest a new club would generate in a city recognized for space travel. Skeptics doubted the city would support a franchise.

The partnership between Schmittou and Davis came at a perfect time for Don Mincher. The forty-six-year-old Huntsville native played parts of thirteen seasons in the Major Leagues before retiring in 1972.

Mincher, a slugging, left-handed first baseman in his playing days, ran a local trophy shop and was itching to return to the game in some capacity. The hometown kid was dubbed "Mr. Baseball" in Huntsville and Schmittou fittingly made him general manager of the new club. Mincher brought immediate local credibility to the team. Mincher was no stranger to new franchises. He was part of two expansion clubs during his career. Hiring a front office was just one order of business in the Minors. Schmittou and Mincher needed a Major League club to bring the Minor Leaguers.

They found one. Huntsville's new baseball stage was perfectly suited for Walt Jocketty, an Oakland A's executive at the time. Oakland's Double-A farm club was just booted from Albany, New York, when the owner of the Eastern League franchise, Ben Bernard, signed a deal with the New York Yankees. Jocketty needed to find a city for his farmhands fast. It all came together in September when he visited Huntsville and signed a two-year working agreement with Schmittou to populate the city with players the next season. Jocketty was also bringing twenty-eight-year-old Brad Fischer, one of Minor League Baseball's winningest managers.

With the instant gratification style of Billy Ball behind them, Oakland's front office was now focused on bolstering their farm system and adding other advancements. In a trade that signified the A's new direction, they netted five players from the Yankees, including four top prospects, in a trade for superstar Rickey Henderson in December. Ten months before, they landed Tim Belcher—baseball's top amateur pitcher—from the Yankees in a controversial free agent compensation pick. They had hired a new, innovative director of player development, Karl Kuehl, and baseball's first full-time psychologist, Harvey Dorfman. Former Major League slugger Bob Watson joined the organization as a Minor League instructor after retiring in 1984. The A's boasted one of baseball's premier farm systems. Many of their Minor Leaguers had tasted championship success in other levels of the system and were slated to play in Double-A in 1985. Baseball insiders forecasted the group of prospects were a few years away from fueling the parent club to championships. Oakland hadn't won a championship since 1974. They finished in fourth place with a record of 77-85 in 1984.

Davis's city, Schmittou's franchise, and Jocketty's farm club were on the brink of a baseball renaissance. Named after the city's connection to space and rocketry, the Huntsville Stars were born in 1985. "That club could have been the best Minor League team ever assembled," said Wayne Giddings, a reliever on the club. The prospect-laden club mauled opposing teams. "We stomped teams right out of the gate," said Charlie O'Brien, a catcher on the club. "We had an incredible team." They swaggered into each city and dominated with a thunderous lineup and strong pitching arms. "We had a lot of power, speed, and great defense," remembered Stan Javier, who manned centerfield for the club. "It was a great team from the beginning." The Stars were the story of the A's organization in 1985. They even had a distinct look. "We were the only A's affiliate that didn't wear green and gold," said Greg Cadaret. "Our team colors were red, white, and blue. We went from white to black shoes."

Brad Fischer understood the caliber of club he was leading. "I told Mincher he may never ever see a team in Huntsville like that one," Fischer recalled. "I still talk about those players. They were the standard for me." Sandy Alderson, general manager, couldn't ignore the reports coming from Rocket City. "The team became almost mythical even during the season," remembered Alderson. Record crowds showed up and players were celebrities in the community. "Huntsville rolled out the red carpet for us," said Ray Thoma, third baseman on the team. "It felt like we were rock stars. They literally gave us the key to the city. We felt like the city was our family." The buzz of Huntsville's baseball carnival spread everywhere. The Stars were the Beatles of Huntsville. "They got more publicity than any Double-A team in the country," the late Bob Mayes, who covered the club for the *Huntsville Times* in 1985, said in 2007. But overtaking John Hart's Charlotte O's, the Double-A farm club of the Baltimore Orioles, and the league's defending champions, would not be easy. It took everything they had.

1

Music City's Field of Dreams

"We felt that by using the entertainment theme of Music City to promote the club, people would show up and they did."—**LARRY SCHMITTOU**, former owner and president, Nashville Sounds, March 2021

July 1984: Larry Schmittou championed baseball in Nashville at every level for all ages, so it was only fitting he wanted a chance to brand Major League Baseball in Music City. Schmittou, a Nashville native, had put the city on the baseball map and was on the verge of bringing Nashville a step closer to an expansion franchise. He not only loved baseball and Nashville, but he was also a marketing genius and shrewd businessman. The forty-four-year-old owner of the Nashville Sounds, the Southern League's most popular franchise, had revived sagging fan interest in Music City. He built the Sounds into one of Minor League Baseball's most successful operations. He was heralded as a stubborn visionary, a baseball savant with a nose for talent, and a daring business mind with a knack for promoting. "He was always smart in knowing the communities he invested in," said John Pruett, former sports editor for the *Huntsville Times*. "He made sure he played all the angles. He was an entrepreneurial genius."

Since 1978, Schmittou popularized pro baseball in Nashville with hard work and innovation. He worked long hours; an associate once claimed Schmittou started the thirty-hour workday. In 1984 Schmittou's product, the Sounds—the Double-A affiliate of the New York Yankees—led the Southern League in attendance for a seventh consecutive season. The Yankees and Nashville had been one of the Minor League's most profitable marriages. They were the league's top attraction that set records at the gate. In 1980 the Sounds drew 575,676 fans at their home field—Herschel Greer Stadium. The figure is the league's highest single season attendance ever. On August 18, 1982, they hosted a crowd of 22,315 for a game, still a league record for a single game. Opposing clubs were pumped to pass through Nashville, too. John Hart, former manager of the Charlotte O's, recalled the anticipation of coming to town. "It was always one of the best trips," said Hart, a former Major League Baseball executive. "The Yankees had so many great players come through there. When you came to Nashville, you always felt like you were the closest to the Major Leagues as you were ever going to get. You put your 'A' game on. They treated you well. It was a great town. They were almost like the outlier of the league. Schmittou ran a first-class operation."

Nashville wasn't the only city experiencing a baseball boom. The popularity of Minor League Baseball was exploding in other parts of the country. There was a revival of interest in the charm and business of the Minors. A big change was that owners were now making a living off the Minor Leagues; owning a club was not just a tax write-off for them. They were becoming more involved in their teams. The business of the Minors was changing. Owners were buying and flipping franchises. Some fans were disenchanted from the 1981 Major League Baseball strike that erased 713 regular season games and paid more attention to the Minor Leagues. In 1983 the Louisville Redbirds, the Triple-A club of the St. Louis Cardinals, became the first Minor League team to draw over one million fans in a season. They boasted a season attendance of 1,052,438, establishing a new Minor League record. The Redbirds filled a void in Louisville, Kentucky, a city facing economic uncertainty and poor optics. Richard L. Walker, in 1982, wrote about the public enthusiasm for the Redbirds in the *Christian Science Monitor*: "The 'Louisville Phenomenon' as it's being called in baseball circles, came at a significant juncture for this 204-year-old city on the Ohio River. Unemployment had been in double digits for months, major local employers such as General Electric and International Harvester announced massive layoffs, and the community was recently ranked

11th in the nation for its dirty air," Walker wrote. National media outlets such as ABC's *Good Morning, America* covered the "Louisville Phenomenon" story.

Schmittou and Nashville were at the forefront of the baseball awakening. "Franchises were starting to sell for some money," said Hart, who managed in the Minor Leagues for six years. "We had never thought there was any money in Minor League Baseball, but owners suddenly started improving facilities and having something going on for fans. Owners were investing in their clubs. Owners started cracking the lid off the perception that there was no money in the Minors. It was no longer just about developing players and being competitive. Owners were buying franchises and selling them for more." On the baseball side, due largely to outrageous free agent salaries, another factor was that Major League clubs were focusing and investing more in their farm systems. More emphasis was being placed on producing big league players and competing through the draft and farm system over trying through free agency. Some Major League owners counted on their farm system to groom talent over engaging in bidding wars with other owners for top players. Paul Owens, a front office executive for the Philadelphia Phillies, described the shift in 1985. "There is more and more emphasis on the Minors today," he said. "Other people are starting to realize what we knew ten years ago—the future is with your farm system. Free agency isn't the answer people thought it would be."

But even during the renaissance and the Sounds' ringing success, attendance at Greer Stadium had declined each year since 1980. By 1984 attendance had dropped to 372,701. They drew only 3,156 for the home opener. Monsoon weather ruined the stadium's playing surface, clubhouses, and offices. The Greenville Braves, the Southern League's new entry, had built a new facility—Greenville Municipal Stadium— that was garnering glowing reviews. Less reporters filled the press box for games at Greer Stadium. The newness of the Sounds was wearing off in Nashville.

Schmittou felt the timing was right to elevate Nashville to a higher level of baseball—Triple-A. He wanted to change it up. The move would generate interest and inch Nashville closer to a Major League expansion team. Given his track record and determination, it was hard to doubt his vision for Nashville's next big splash. Schmittou's award-winning formula had turned Nashville into a baseball hotbed, but his success was predictable. He demonstrated a golden touch early in life.

Growing up, Schmittou, the youngest of five children, fell in love with baseball while watching the Nashville Volunteers, a Double-A club, at Sulphur Dell with his mother, Jane Ann. In fact, when Schmittou was born on July 19, 1940, Jane Ann named him after Larry Gilbert, the Vols' winning manager. Schmittou played baseball and coached around Nashville since he was a kid. He was a winner early. The hometown prodigy, in his teens, was already earning a reputation as a bright baseball mind around summer leagues in the late 1950s. He had more irons in the fire than a blacksmith. After playing in a game, he rushed to the next baseball diamond to serve as a coach. He pitched for Cohn High School in West Nashville and graduated in 1958. Schmittou started a family the following year. On November 28, 1959, Schmittou, nineteen, married Shirley Ann Reynolds, eighteen, his high school sweetheart. Schmittou, right away, took his family on a baseball bliss.

Schmittou began coaching when he was a pitcher in his junior year at Cohn High and boasted an unofficial record of 420-74 in amateur leagues. "From Little League baseball to Babe Ruth and Connie Mack leagues, he coached great teams that won championships," said Skip Nipper, a Nashville baseball historian. Schmittou, considered a winning sandlot tutor, had graduated from neighboring George Peabody College in 1962. Wayne Garland, a former Major League pitcher, grew up in Nashville and played intermittently for many of Schmittou's amateur clubs before being drafted in 1968. Garland, who was part of baseball's first free agent class in 1976 when he signed an unprecedented ten-year, $2 million contract with the Cleveland Indians, remembered Schmittou's bright baseball mind, dedication, and long practices. "He was the epitome of amateur baseball in Nashville," Garland said. Garland said Schmittou, a high schooler at the time, used to drive his station wagon around the neighborhood to pick up players and take them to practice.

"There were nine or ten of us in the car," Garland remembered. The equipment was stuffed in the back. After practice, he dropped them off back home. Like Schmittou, Garland attended Cohn High. He said Schmittou was known for hustling to find players to improve his clubs. "He was one of the first in the area to recruit players," Garland noted. "He got the best high school players in Nashville to play for his Connie Mack team. He had the best players in the city."

Playing under Schmittou's winning hand required sacrifice. Baseball was life, especially in the heart of the summer when playing four games a day was not uncommon. He himself invested a great deal of time in the sport. "He wasn't an easy guy to play for," Garland said. "Even in Little League, he demanded a lot from his players. Our practices were four or five hours long. We'd practice, take a break, and practice more. If you wanted to play for Nashville's best baseball coach, you played for Schmittou. If you wanted to play for Nashville's best team, you played for him. You had to commit yourself to play all the time. If you were not serious about baseball, you had no business playing for him." Garland noted that Schmittou was also savvy at finding sponsors for his teams.

While attending Peabody College, he worked at the Ford Glass Plant to support his family. He also coached basketball and football at Goodlettsville High School. Schmittou's coaching prowess sparked the interest of Vanderbilt University, Nashville's prestigious and private institution of higher learning founded in 1873. But nothing was prestigious about Vanderbilt's baseball team. Jess Neely, Vanderbilt's ambitious new athletic director, inherited a neglected program and heard about Schmittou's winning reputation. On February 7, 1968, Neely made the twenty-seven-year-old the first ever fulltime baseball coach at the university. Neely wanted to jumpstart the decaying program. "Larry's reputation in the amateur ranks got him the Vanderbilt job," said Nipper.

Schmittou understood he was taking over a withered baseball program with an embarrassing 18-42 record over the last three seasons. The university did not offer any baseball scholarships to recruits in the highly competitive Southeastern Conference. The Commodores fielded a team only because they were required to have one. "Vanderbilt baseball did not have a great following back then like today," said Nipper. Schmittou, being at the forefront of Nashville baseball for so many years, recognized the program was in much worse condition than even Neely realized. Being a "bird dog" scout for the Cleveland Indians since 1963 required him to evaluate players at Vanderbilt's McGugin Field, and while attending Peabody College, he came to the university occasionally to throw batting practice. He knew how bad they were.

He was familiar with some of the Vanderbilt players from coaching summer leagues. "I was minding my own business coaching at Goodlettsville in February of 1968 and Mr. Neely showed up," recalled Schmittou. "He told me he'd like for me to be his new baseball coach, and I asked him, 'Why would I want to do that? Y'all are awful.'" Neely agreed but charmed Schmittou with promised support. "You're right, but with my help, you can correct it," Neely told him. The program was the laughingstock of the Southeastern Conference (SEC). "When I took the Vandy job, we had no scholarships, while most SEC teams had nineteen," Schmittou said. "Finally, we worked our way up to three scholarships to divide up. I had to count on a lot of walk-ons." He could count the fans in the stands at McGugin Field, too. The home field of the Commodores was empty. "We didn't have many people come to the games," said Schmittou. "There were four people in the stands one day—my wife, daughter, and two traveling salesmen. The salesmen left town and left us with two."

Schmittou created momentum from scratch. He lived up to his sparkling reputation and brought respectability to the Vandy program. The Commodores greatly benefited from his leadership and bright baseball mind. In 1969 Schmittou, nicknamed "Smokey" by his players, led the Commodores to their first winning season since 1955 with a 21-18 record. They improved again the following season with a strong record of 24-16 under Schmittou, who also served as Vanderbilt's head football recruiter. Before resigning as head baseball coach in 1979, he led the Commodores to 306 wins over ten seasons, including four consecutive divisional titles from 1971 to 1974 and two SEC championships.

Schmittou was named the SEC's Baseball Coach of the Year in 1973 and 1974. "We have been able to come up with some non-scholarship players, particularly some top prospects who are willing to come at their own expense and wait around until someone leaves and money is available for them," Schmittou said in 1974. When Schmittou had taken over, he suggested he would have a contender in "three or four years." The prediction was once described as "Schmittou's Folly." "There is a great deal of Vanderbilt baseball lore . . . but it's all bad—or at least humorous—until things began to happen in March of 1968," wrote Jimmy Davy of *The Tennessean* in 1974. On course with his track record, Schmittou had built the fledgling program into a winner. "So many guys who played on our Connie Mack teams followed him to Vanderbilt," said Garland. "He was the foundation of Vanderbilt's program today."

As Schmittou's family was expanding, his expenses were growing. The thirty-eight-year-old husband and father of four needed to earn more money to support his growing family. The National Collegiate Athletic Association had recently ruled that colleges could no longer employ full-time recruiters. The decision impacted his earnings. "They were going to have to cut my salary 33 percent, and I had four kids with a fifth on the way," Schmittou said in 1990. "I had no money." While weighing career options, Schmittou was fascinated by rejuvenated interest in Minor League Baseball in some parts of the country. "Minor League Baseball was becoming a spectator sport that could pay for itself," recalled Schmittou. "For many, many years, the Minor Leagues had been going out of style. Owners were going broke." The new wave intrigued Schmittou, and he was up for a new challenge.

In 1976 Schmittou, while still coaching for Vanderbilt, was compelled to ride the wave and bring a Minor League team to Nashville. But some felt his optimism about baseball returning was misplaced. After all, the Nashville Vols of the South Atlantic League, were a financial flop and folded in 1963, a week after the season ended because of poor attendance and financial woes. The Vols were such a disappointment at the gate that many insiders thought a pro baseball club would never return. There were doubts about Nashville's passion to support professional sports. The Dixie Flyers, Nashville's hockey team that played in the Eastern Hockey League, disbanded in 1971 from lack of fan support. Despite the doubters, the persistent and stubborn Schmittou formed a group of investors to finance the return of Minor League Baseball. "I always knew that if Nashville had a team and a stadium, we could draw enough fans to pay our bills," said Schmittou. "I would have stayed at Vanderbilt, if I could have made enough money to raise my family."

Country music money funded Schmittou's baseball vision for Music City. "We felt that by using the entertainment theme of Music City to promote the club, people would show up and they did," recalled Schmittou. Investors like Conway Twitty, the late country music legend, bought into Schmittou's plan to parlay music and baseball in Nashville. Schmittou had worked with Twitty's son, Jimmy Jenkins, in a Vanderbilt baseball camp. Twitty's participation was crucial. "It could not have been done without Conway," said Schmittou. "I drew up a limited partnership agreement and he took 20 percent and led me to other investors." Twitty's country music peers Cal Smith, Larry Gatlin, Jerry Reed, and Richard Sterban of the Oak Ridge Boys suddenly followed suit as stakeholders and the Nashville Baseball Club was born. Schmittou and company needed to get to work right away. They were responsible for coming up with the money to build a new stadium for the club. Sulphur Dell, where the Vols had played since 1901, was demolished in 1969.

Schmittou, president of the club, led the charge on a new stadium. He worked long hours, regularly putting in eighteen- to twenty-hour workdays. "He was a visionary and not afraid to take a chance," said Nipper. The community bought into Schmittou's plan. The family of the late Herschel Greer, the former president of the Vols, contributed $50,000 in Greer's memory to help build the stadium. Schmittou named the new stadium in Greer's honor. "A new park was built in Jackson, Mississippi, and I went there to look at it to get some ideas," recalled Schmittou. "I told a local architect to put together a design for the stadium." The city had cautioned Schmittou they were not going to contribute any funds toward the construction of the park, but they offered him some land to build the ballpark on.

City officials approved Schmittou to build the stadium on Fort Negley Park in South Nashville. The city had shut down the Civil War fort after decades of neglect. After evaluating the land, however, the initial consensus was the parking lot was not big enough to accommodate bigger crowds. But Schmittou settled on the site. "It wasn't my preferred site, but it was my only alternative," he said. "I knew parking was going to be a huge issue." The stadium almost never happened as Schmittou's group was shy $200,000 to start construction in August 1977, but the city loaned them the rest. Schmittou, who took a $100,000 loan on his house to contribute to the $1 million stadium, finally broke ground on August 26, 1977. The 6,500-seat stadium was slated to be completed by March 1, 1978. Before the stadium was ready, Schmittou had already been a carnival barker for Music City's new baseball dream. He sold 2,100 season tickets at $200 each. "I had a builder that worked with me, and some great citizens of Nashville donated their services to help us build it," Schmittou said.

Schmittou hoped to land a Triple-A club in the American Association right off the bat, but there were more expansion opportunities in Double-A with the Southern League, and he lured the Cincinnati Reds of the National League. Schmittou inked a three-year working agreement with the Reds on September 20, 1977; and Nashville became the home of Cincinnati's Double-A farm club with a 144-game Southern League schedule for the 1978 season. "When he and Farrell Owens, the club's general manager, visited the baseball winter meetings to promote Nashville, they only had a room," remembered Nipper. "They walked around distributing their contact information inside each of the club's mailboxes. Sheldon Bender, the Reds' farm director, suddenly called and said they might be interested in moving their Double-A farm club from Three Rivers, Canada, to Nashville, and they struck a deal." Playing in the Southern League attracted Bender, who was also impressed with Schmittou's ambitious ownership group. Moving the farm club from Canada to Nashville would give the Reds an opportunity to monitor farmhands more closely. Plus, a new stadium was a significant factor. "Nashville offers us a good, energetic ownership," Bender said at the time. "It offers us a facility which I'm certain will be excellent. It offers us a warm weather climate we've been missing in Canada. And it offers us the competition of a strong league in the Southern League."

Schmittou's dream was coming together. He landed Cincinnati and was building a new stadium in his hometown all while fulfilling his coaching duties at Vanderbilt. Now the franchise needed a name. By late September 1977, after the Nashville Baseball Club promoted a "Name the Team" contest with hundreds of fan entries, a thirteen-member panel selected "Sounds" as the name for the new club. It captured the Music City theme. On April 26, 1978, the Nashville Sounds, donning red, white, and blue uniforms, played at their new home—Herschel Greer Stadium—in front of a crowd of 8,156. Schmittou's vision had materialized, but his celebration was subdued. A day before the Sounds opened their new stadium, Jane Ann, Schmittou's mother, passed away. She was eighty-two. (Egbert Schmittou, Larry's father, a disabled World War I veteran, died on September 3, 1986, at the age of ninety-two.)

The Sounds were a big hit at the gate. They led the Minor Leagues in attendance in 1978, drawing 380,159 fans in their inaugural season despite a losing record of 64-77 and finishing fourth in the league's Western Division. Partnering with large local corporations, Schmittou's clever, innovative ballpark promotions with a country music theme to enhance fan experience attracted fans to Greer Stadium. The Sounds were becoming the model franchise fast. Schmittou was known to mingle in the stands with fans. Because of Nashville's impressive inaugural season, he was recognized after the season and swept every award for Minor League executives. The National Association of Professional Baseball Leagues (NAPBL) awarded Schmittou with the Larry MacPhail Trophy for having Minor League Baseball's top operation in 1978. The *Sporting News* named Schmittou the Class AA Executive of the Year, and the NAPBL crowned him the Southern League's Executive of the Year. "Nashville's success was truly remarkable," Bobby Bragan, president of the NAPBL, said during baseball's winter meetings in 1978. "Everybody in the baseball world was talking about Nashville this summer, and they're still talking about Nashville here at the winter meetings. There was never much question about who would win this award." Schmittou opted to resign from Vanderbilt after the season to focus fulltime on running the Sounds. Equally impressive as Schmittou's baseball savvy as a coach was his ability to make baseball attractive to fans. He proved it in Nashville. "Schmittou founded the Nashville Sounds with not much more than a stubborn streak and a dream. He fought bureaucratic battles, hustled and huckstered for financing and almost mystically breathed professional baseball back to life in Music City," wrote Larry Woody of *The Tennessean* in 1997. The Sounds hosted "Larry Schmittou Appreciation Night" on August 31, 1978.

On September 2, 1979, the Sounds became the first Minor League club in modern history to draw more than a half million fans in a season. Despite losing four home dates from rainouts, Nashville drew 504,401 in sixty-six regular-season home games, breaking the record held by the Hawaiian Islanders in 1970 when they drew 467,217 fans in seventy home dates. On the field, Nashville won the Southern League crown. Despite the dream season at the gate and in the standings, Nashville's partnership with Cincinnati ended after the season. By May Schmittou and the Reds decided to part ways after two seasons. The Reds, a National League franchise, refused to use a designated hitter in games because they wanted their pitchers to get used to hitting as they would under league rules. But opposing clubs used the designated hitter against them. Schmittou felt the handicap cost the Sounds dozens of wins. "It put us at a disadvantage," he said.

A blockbuster announcement came after the season. Schmittou struck a deal with the Yankees, an American League club that used a designated hitter. On September 11,1979, Nashville signed a two-year working agreement with New York. The Yankees were moving their Double-A club from West Haven, Connecticut, to Nashville. New York's farm system was loaded. In 1979 all five of the Yankees' farm teams had winning seasons and finished in first place. New York sweetened the deal by throwing in an exhibition game with the Yankees at Greer Stadium during the 1980 season. The partnership between the defending world champions and baseball's rising promoter didn't disappoint. The franchise celebrated their best run with the Yankees from 1980 to 1984. The team boasted a regular season record of 417-306 (.577), winning two Western Division titles and one championship in 1982. They were the league's feature attraction, boasting the highest attendance since they arrived in 1980. They were one of the most successful alliances in the Minors. The Sounds, highlighted by future big leaguers Don Mattingly, Bob Tewksbury, Jose Rijo, Steve Balboni, and Mike Pagliarulo, had made the postseason every season since joining forces with the Yankees.

Business, meanwhile, was booming, and the country music ownership group expanded and purchased four more clubs, with Nashville becoming the flagship. Nashville was selected to host baseball's winter meetings in 1983 at the Opryland Hotel. "The story of the Sounds' impressive Greer Stadium facility and their spectacular box office success already is familiar throughout the world of sports, and the selection of our town as the site for the important off-season convention adds luster to Nashville's image as a baseball hotbed and tourist attraction," wrote John Bibb of *The Tennessean* in 1982. To accommodate more fans, Greer Stadium's capacity increased to sixteen thousand. Expanding Nashville's sports landscape further, Schmittou's group brought professional hockey back to the city. The South Stars of the Central Hockey League, the top club of the National Hockey League's Minnesota North Stars, started playing in Nashville in 1981. The club joined the Atlantic Coast Hockey League the following season, before Schmittou sold the team in 1983. Schmittou's plan was to build the South Stars into a model franchise like he did the Sounds. As Schmittou promoted Nashville to lure other sports franchises, not everyone was a fan of his style. Bringing a sports franchise required him to negotiate and seek approval from Nashville's forty-member Metro Council. He rubbed some of them the wrong way. His ultimatums irked some council members. Some of them considered him a slick-talking wheeler-dealer who always wanted his way. But even Schmittou's staunchest critics respected what he had accomplished. He was thick-skinned and never unraveled under criticism.

What Schmittou was accomplishing in Nashville was garnering interest nationwide. He made the Sounds a model Minor League club and his name was buzzing around baseball. Major League owners sought his golden touch. In February 1983, the Texas Rangers named Schmittou, forty-two, the vice president and director of marketing. "The Texas Rangers job is the only one in big league baseball that offers enough appeal at this time for me to leave Nashville," said Schmittou, who moved to Arlington, Texas, but remained president of the Sounds. While Schmittou was earning more money than he ever had and gaining notoriety around baseball as a top marketing executive and owner, he never abandoned his plan for Nashville. As popular as the Sounds had become, he always wanted the highest level of baseball in Nashville.

He found an opportunity to elevate Nashville to Triple-A in June 1984, when he learned of a struggling franchise in Evansville, Indiana, for sale. The Evansville Triplets, the Triple-A club of the Detroit Tigers, were losing interest in the city. The city struggled to support the farm club that was losing money fast. The Triplets, a part of the American Association, played at Bosse Field. After arriving to Evansville in 1970, the Triplets averaged only 1,300 fans per game in 1984 and made money in only four of fifteen years. The franchise was $30,000 in the red. In 1982 the parent-club, the Tigers, came to Evansville for an exhibition game and only 2,623 fans showed up. While the Tigers were roaring their way to a World Series title in 1984, the Triplets were purring in Evansville. The popularity and success of the Tigers was not manifesting in Evansville. Schmittou had made offers to purchase the franchise before, but the owners weren't ready to close the chapter on Evansville. The timing was right this time. Backed by stakeholders, Schmittou purchased the Triplets in July and planned on moving the Triple-A franchise to Nashville for the 1985 season. Nashville was inheriting Evansville's working agreement with Detroit. "We hosted Double-A until a Triple-A opportunity arose, which happened when the Evansville franchise was up for sale," recalled Schmittou. "We purchased Evansville with the sole purpose of moving that club to Nashville."

The proposed move would impact the league and other clubs. With the arrival of Detroit's Triple-A farmhands and switching from the Southern League to the American Association, the fate of Nashville's existing Double-A franchise needed to be determined. The move also meant the Southern League would be losing its top attraction—the Sounds. Elevating Nashville would end the franchise's five-year partnership with the Yankees. New York already had a successful Triple-A affiliate in Columbus, Ohio, so they severed ties after the 1984 season. The move first needed approval from league directors.

Early indications were that Nashville and Evansville would swap franchises and leagues. The rumor was that Nashville's Double-A franchise would move to Evansville and stay in the Southern League, and Nashville would host the Evansville franchise and play in the American Association. Some league executives, however, opposed Evansville joining the league. Bob Willis, general manager of the Orlando Twins, was one of them. Traveling in the Southern League was notoriously difficult, highlighted by long bus rides from city to city. He thought the fifteen-hour Florida-to-Indiana road trip would be too much. Nashville was already a twelve-hour bus ride for Orlando. Based on the Triplets being on life support in Evansville, some doubted the city could support a Double-A club. So, the swap never materialized.

To Schmittou—as far as he was concerned—the important move was complete. He was bringing Nashville a higher brand of baseball, another stepping-stone toward his dream of landing a Major League franchise. "The successful operation of a Triple-A team definitely enhances our chances of securing a big league team in Nashville within the next decade," he told reporters during a press conference announcing the purchase on July 11, 1984. Detroit's incoming farm club inherited the "Sounds" name when they arrived. The Tigers were Nashville's third Major League partnership since 1978, when the Sounds were born. Although Schmittou and Nashville benefited from the purchase, the loss was a blow to the Southern League. The league would be losing the Sounds, Schmittou, and Nashville. "It's not exactly good news for our league. Nashville is the No. 1 Double-A franchise in the Minors and it will definitely hurt to lose it," Jimmy Bragan, former Southern League commissioner, said in 1984. It cost Schmittou about $250,000 in compensation for the league to approve the relocation. "The league was never unreasonable," recalled Schmittou. "That's just the way the Minor Leagues work. They didn't want to lose Nashville."

The league and Schmittou still needed to figure out what to do with Nashville's existing Double-A franchise. Schmittou preferred to keep his franchise of seven years in the Southern League.

"He wanted Triple-A baseball in Nashville, but he wanted to keep his Double-A franchise," the late Bob Mayes, who covered the Huntsville Stars for the *Huntsville Times* in 1985, said in 2007. Down South, in Huntsville, Alabama, Joe W. Davis, the city's mayor, wanted a professional baseball club for Rocket City. Whether Schmittou could transfer the franchise to Huntsville was another story. "I needed a home for my franchise," Schmittou said. Davis wanted a team for his city.

2

The Phenom

"It was something out of *Field of Dreams*, in the scene where the long lines of cars begin pulling off the interstate to get a look at what has come to play ball in the corn-field-turned diamond."—**JOHN ERARDI**, *Cincinnati Enquirer*, 1992

February 1984: The merging of twenty-two-year-old Tim Belcher, baseball's top amateur pitching phenom, and the filthy rich New York Yankees was sure to be a sexy alliance. The flame-throwing right-hander from Mount Vernon Nazarene College in Mount Vernon, Ohio, had been the first selection of the summer and winter Major League drafts. The Yankees were one of baseball's most profitable superpowers on the brink of new levels of riches. WPIX, the television home of the Yankees since 1951, was becoming a rising superstation, bringing the team into millions of homes around the country, earning the franchise millions. The demand was such that Yankees games were carried via satellite to cable stations around the country, strengthening owner George Steinbrenner's empire. Belcher seemed destined to become the centerpiece prince of New York's starting rotation. He reminded many scouts of pitching great Tom Seaver. Like Seaver, the thick-thighed Belcher was right-handed and dragged his knee on the mound when he finished his windup. He dropped so low and drove so hard, his knee bumped the ground when he fired a pitch. The windup generated explosive power behind his pitches. The possibilities for Belcher and the Yankees materialized when New York held the first pick of baseball's January winter draft in 1984 and selected the six-foot-three, 220-pound sensation.

Despite drawing the spotlight of being a first pick, Belcher only recently had pulled scouts. But they stalked him late, hard, and fast. The country boy from Sparta, a tiny town of 250 people about six miles north of the geographical center of Ohio, Belcher was raised in a farming community. In fact, he worked on several nearby farms as a youth. His family home was on five acres, and he helped care for his grandfather's race horses on the property. Livestock surrounded him. Some rural youth couldn't participate in sports because of demanding house chores, but Don and Gladys, Tim's parents, encouraged their children to have a life away from the home. Growing up, Belcher, a fan of the Cincinnati Reds, wanted to take over for his idol—catcher Johnny Bench. The Reds played 150 miles from his home. The Southern Morrow County teen preferred being a position player over pitching in high school. After leading Highland High School in rebounds on the basketball court, he transitioned into baseball season every spring and played shortstop for the varsity squad. He hit with power. "I hated pitching in high school, I wanted to play every day," Belcher said in 1983. Even though Belcher pitched some, he was the best high school hitter in North Central Ohio, boasting a .460 batting average in his junior and senior year for the Scots. But no scouts or Division I colleges showed interest in the first-team All-County shortstop.

Sam Riggleman, the head baseball coach for Mount Vernon Nazarene, a tiny nearby NAIA college, was the only one coming to Highland to see him. Riggleman liked Belcher's bat and recruited him to be his third baseman, but also knew he was available to pitch occasionally. The NAIA, National Association of Intercollegiate Athletics, was far from a hotbed for future Major Leaguers, but Belcher accepted a partial scholarship and attended Mount Vernon in the fall of 1980. "I ended up going there from necessity, really," remembered Belcher, an instructor for the Cleveland Indians today. "I didn't have a lot of other opportunities." The college didn't offer any full or half scholarships. A Mount Vernon player had never been drafted by a Major League team.

Late in the summer of 1980, Belcher's promise to Mount Vernon was quickly tested. While pitching in the Ohio State Legion Baseball

Tournament, he attracted the interest of a Division I program. Jerry France, Ohio University's head baseball coach, began pursuing him. "I pitched a couple complete games and we ended up winning the state tournament in Athens, Ohio," remembered Belcher, who posted an 8-1 record for Ashley American, Ohio's American Legion champions. "Ohio University was out there, and France asked my high school coach about me coming there to pitch on a partial scholarship. But I had already told Mount Vernon I was coming. Before that, I had already made inquiries to Ohio University, and many other colleges, and never received a response. They didn't recruit me until very late in the summer. But it was too late." But France persisted and told Belcher he could get out of his promise to Mount Vernon and play for a Division I school, but he stuck with his plans. "I told him, 'No, I'll fulfill my promise to Riggleman at Mount Vernon,'" recalled Belcher. "I don't think it would have turned out much better."

While Belcher could have made a Division I team as a non-scholarship, walk-on, Mount Vernon was a good fit for the business administration major. The college, a two-hundred-acre campus with only one thousand students, was only twelve miles from his home, so he commuted every morning. The intimacy of Mount Vernon benefited him in the classroom and on the diamond. He enjoyed the personal attention. Belcher played third base and pitched during his freshman year at Mount Vernon. Playing third base for the Cougars, Belcher batted .270 with five homers. On the mound, he was 4-4 with a 5.59 earned run average. By the end of the season, Belcher was the No. 2 starter in the rotation and showing more interest in being on the mound. But some wondered if he had the temperament for a pitcher. He was a fierce competitor, and it was hard for him to conceal his emotions. When he didn't excel, he got down on himself and was angry after losses. After his freshman season, the nineteen-year-old attended a tryout hosted by Reds' scout Gene Bennett in Piqua. Belcher was clocked in the high eighties, and the Reds showed interest. Inspired by the tryout, Belcher told Riggleman he wanted to focus on pitching. "By the time my sophomore year rolled around, I started getting attention from pro scouts as a pitcher," said Belcher. "That's all I did after that." As a sophomore at Mount Vernon, Belcher was 5-4, fanning seventy-nine in seventy-seven innings. Scouts for the Reds and Los Angeles Dodgers were coming around to see him. Figuring they had a local phenom on their hands, the Reds wanted to keep Belcher a secret like a one hundred dollar bill on a lonely sidewalk.

Belcher drew a wider audience of scouts soon. While compiling a 9-8 record and 4.65 earned run average in his first two years at Mount Vernon, he got his big break before his junior season. In October 1982 Belcher drove to a tryout in Columbus for the U.S. Pan American team at Ohio State. There, he was not just performing to make the Pan Am team. Big league scouts were on hand with radar guns to scope talent. A Cincinnati scout pulled Belcher aside and encouraged him not to throw hard in front of other scouts, but he seized the moment. He fired a fastball that hit over ninety miles per hour on the radar gun in front of the scouts in forty-degree weather. Dozens of perked-up scouts immediately fell in love with Belcher's arm and were on his trail. Belcher suddenly became the kid every scout was curious about because they never had heard of him. The freshness of Belcher's lively arm intrigued them. He never had a chance to abuse his arm in high school like other kids did. He was a late bloomer with a ripe arm. "They viewed Tim as a Cadillac that had hardly been out of the garage," Riggleman once said.

Before Belcher's junior season in 1983, scouts hunted Riggleman down for Mount Vernon's schedule to see the fireballer. Belcher's first game of the season was in Hanover, Indiana, and as he walked off the bus, ten scouts were waiting. Scouts from all over the country descended on the NAIA school and swarmed the stands. The presence of so many scouts rattled Belcher early on, but he fought through the nervousness. He fired a no-hitter and struck out eighteen batters in a 16–0 mauling of Kenyon College on April 5, 1983. Besides a heater, Belcher featured a slurve and changeup in his arsenal. By May over fifty scouts were showing up to see him. The remarkable story of a golden-armed, pitching phenom wooing scouts from a tiny Ohio college was spreading fast. "It was something out of *Field of Dreams*, in the scene where the long lines of cars begin pulling off the interstate to get a look at what has come to play ball in the corn-field-turned diamond," wrote John Erardi of the *Cincinnati Enquirer* in 1992.

After opening his junior season 1-4, Belcher finished with a 5-4 record and 2.86 earned run average for the 14-14 Cougars. He battled inconsistency and wildness. But Belcher's ninety-three strikeouts in sixty-six and a third innings made scouts overlook his less than spectacular record. They wanted his arm. He finished the season striking out fifty-one in his final thirty-one innings, allowing only one run. In a matter of months, Belcher, who just hoped to get drafted going into the season, became the top prospect in the country leading up to Major League Baseball's June Amateur Draft. Belcher sensed he could be picked early in the draft when scouts started asking him for his price tag to sign. He wanted a six-figure signing bonus. All things were pointing to Belcher leaving Mount Vernon after his junior year and signing with a Major League club. The NAIA All-American was anxious to start his professional career.

As May gave way to June, the Minnesota Twins were preparing to pick first to open the June 6 draft. Baseball insiders felt the talent available in the 1983 draft was mediocre. *Baseball America*'s predraft scouting report on Belcher opined that "he's the only pitcher in the draft who can really throw the ball by a hitter." Central scouting advised that Belcher was the best player available. The Twins were keeping tabs on Belcher. He pitched in the Springfield-Dayton semipro league after his junior season, and Floyd Baker, Minnesota's Ohio scout, trailed him. Baker said Belcher was the best pitcher he scouted in ten years. Belcher was already 2-0 in the summer and mowing down batters. George Brophy, Twins' farm director, had seen Belcher at Mount Vernon on June 1 and was smitten by his arm.

Minnesota couldn't pass on Belcher. They made him the No. 1 pick in the draft and secured the rights to sign him. But their brief public partnership on June 6 was all for show. Belcher and the Twins were never on the same page in negotiations from the jump. Minnesota played more hardball than Belcher expected and preferred. It demoralized him. The Twins were in turmoil and owner Calvin Griffith was cutting costs. The Twins weren't drawing any fans at the Metrodome and had the third lowest attendance in the big leagues. Griffith was blaming the flaws of the Metrodome—Minnesota's home field—local media, and a dead business community for the club's decline. What Minnesota offered Belcher was a faster route to the big leagues because they were rushing prospects. But Belcher maintained that if he couldn't agree to terms with them, he would return to Mount Vernon for his senior year. "A fast-track to the big leagues was attractive for a young kid like me coming from a small college," said Belcher. "But I wasn't going to sell my soul for being a No. 1 pick and take a third of what first picks were getting at the time." Belcher felt right away the dysfunction of the frugal Twins. "I think they thought a small-town, country boy would take any money they offered," Belcher said. "They had no money. They also drafted Billy Swift and Oddibe McDowell that year but didn't sign any of us. It was kind of the end of the Calvin Griffith ownership period there."

Since No. 1 pick Darryl Strawberry received a signing bonus of $225,000 from the New York Mets in 1980, Belcher figured landing a bonus of somewhere between $100,000 and $200,000 was fair. But Bryan Oelkers, Minnesota's No. 1 choice the previous season, signed for only $69,500, the largest bonus the club had ever paid. The disenchanted Belcher started traveling with the U.S. Pan Am team in July and hired Chicago agent Scott Boras to evaluate any offers. But Belcher made it clear that Boras was acting as a lawyer and not his agent. Having an agent would have disqualified him from returning to Mount Vernon for his senior year if he didn't sign. The Twins took offense to Belcher bringing Boras into the mix, and the distrust grew. Belcher wanted more than the three-payment $120,000 Minnesota offered under the stern hand of Griffith. Minnesota claimed they were so poor they needed to borrow the money to sign Belcher. The distance between both sides grew and the negotiations fell apart. By September the Twins cut their offer to $60,000 and eventually disappeared from

Belcher's trail. Minnesota never offered Belcher more than $120,000. "The relationship soured quickly and ended unceremoniously," recalled Belcher. He became only the second No. 1 selection not to sign in the history of the draft. Not signing Belcher was yet another publicity blunder for the Twins. They were ridiculed for not signing or trading him in the spring at the very least. The Chicago White Sox had made Danny Goodwin the first pick of the 1971 draft but never signed him. Belcher came close to being drafted by his favorite team—the Reds. They picked after Minnesota and selected Kurt Stillwell, a high school shortstop from Thousand Oaks, California. Stillwell, eighteen, turned down a four-year baseball scholarship from Stanford University to sign with the Reds.

Belcher never enrolled for his senior year at Mount Vernon. Boras initially contended that Belcher could attend classes at Mount Vernon and still be eligible to sign only if he didn't accept a baseball scholarship. But the commissioner's office ruled in September that Belcher needed to be out of school to be eligible to sign with Minnesota and be out of school for 120 days to be available for the January winter draft. He was still eligible to sign with the Twins until January 9, but it never happened. They had stopped communicating for months. The discontent between both sides reached newspapers and Brophy left Belcher some departing blows: "If you ask me, I think Mr. Belcher has a fear of failure," Brophy said after not signing him. "When we got our offer up to $120,000, he still wouldn't sign. He pitches better with his tongue than his arm."

But many clubs were in love with his arm and eyeing him for the January 17, 1984, winter draft, when 104 players would be available. The consensus was that Belcher would be picked first again. Belcher knew that, too and laid low until the draft, working out at Mount Vernon, where dozens of scouts came to see him. They wanted to hear his side of the story on what happened with Minnesota. He was confident he made the right choice in not signing. As a result of a drawing in New York a few days before the draft, the Yankees were awarded the first pick. New York sent five top scouts to evaluate Belcher. As expected, the Yankees drafted Belcher first and had him signed by February. New York gave Belcher a signing bonus of $125,000, and he was scheduled to report to Fort Lauderdale and the Class A Florida State League on February 28. "The Yankees came to one of my workouts at Mount Vernon," said Belcher. "They drafted and signed me quick. Going in, they knew what they were going to spend. Signing me quickly probably was a mistake, because when they signed me, I had to go on one of their Minor League rosters."

Signing Belcher too fast haunted New York a week later. The steamy romance between baseball's top phenom and the storied Yankees was short-lived. A new free-agent system that owners and players negotiated into baseball's collective bargaining agreement on July 31, 1981, to halt the midseason work stoppage came out of nowhere to kill their plans. As Belcher celebrated his new signing bonus and new life with the Yankees, free agent Tom Underwood, a left-handed reliever for the Oakland A's in 1983, signed with the Baltimore Orioles on February 7. Because Underwood departed Oakland as a free agent, the two-year-old free agent compensation system made the A's eligible for a compensation pick from a pool of unprotected players established by each club. The deadline for New York to submit their list of twenty-six protected players was January 13. The players New York protected would be immune from being selected from the compensation pool. Since free agency was born in 1976, the topic of free agent compensation was always a polarizing bargaining topic between owners and players. Owners demanded a compensation system for clubs losing players via free agency to help subsidize the loss. But the players adamantly opposed the owner's proposal, and the disagreement eventually provoked the 1981 midseason strike.

The spotlight came on free agent compensation on February 8, when Oakland shocked the baseball world and selected Belcher from a pool of 250 unprotected players. Oakland's selection of Belcher blindsided the Yankees and Belcher himself. Oakland had never sent any scouts to watch Belcher at Mount Vernon. He was made available to the A's because New York technically left him unprotected after signing him.

The system essentially allowed Oakland to land Belcher for Underwood, a thirty-year-old reliever. Underwood played only one more season. "The Yankees didn't realize they needed to protect him," said Walt Jocketty, the A's farm director at the time, "so, we were very fortunate to slip in there and get him." The Yankees were pissed off and filed a formal protest for losing their top prospect without warning. "We intend to pursue the legality of the selection of Belcher," Murray Cook, general manager of the Yankees, said at the time. "We feel the selection should be overturned." Making matters worse for New York was the fact that they were still responsible for Belcher's signing bonus. Losing Belcher shook the Yankees front office, and a furious Steinbrenner demanded answers immediately. "Tim was not even in the organization when the list was submitted," Joe Safety, New York's director of public relations, said in 1984. "It's grossly unfair. We are victims of an unfair compensation system."

It was hard to argue with Safety. When the Yankees drafted Belcher on January 17, they had already submitted their list of twenty-six protected players on January 13. The list was final. New York didn't know they needed to protect Belcher from the pool, given they just signed him on February 1. "I signed, but the Yankees already had their protected list in," recalled Belcher. "As soon as my name appeared on the roster, I became eligible for the compensation pool draft." Baseball insiders chimed in on Oakland's shrewd move. "That might be the biggest steal since the Brinks job," Gary Hughes, a scout for the Yankees said at the time. Phil Seghi, general manager of the Cleveland Indians, discussed the bad optics of losing a No. 1 pick. "That's the sort of public relations nightmare no team wants," Seghi said. "Imagine us losing, well, the caliber of a player like Bert Blyleven or Andre Thornton. It would be a disaster."

The White Sox pulled a similar move to the A's when they lost reliever Dennis Lamp to free agency a few weeks earlier. Lamp signed with the Toronto Blue Jays on January 10, and the White Sox proceeded to grab Tom Seaver, a three-time Cy Young Award winner, from the compensation pool on January 20. He was property of the Mets, but they left him unprotected. Oakland could have technically picked Seaver from the pool. Chicago, after selecting Seaver, had no way of protecting him by the time Oakland selected on February 8. But Oakland wanted the best player available, Belcher. Belcher, meanwhile, weighed his options. "There may be an opportunity for me to file a grievance if they don't reverse the decision," Belcher told WOUB radio in 1984. "I signed a contract to play for the New York Yankees and I haven't been given the opportunity to do that. There may be some action I can take with the help of the players' association."

Belcher never filed a grievance, but everyone agreed the system needed overhaul. Oakland's opportunity to scoop Belcher was not what owners and players intended when they came up with the idea of a pool. While owners had insisted on free agent compensation, the new system they pushed hard for was backfiring and bringing division among them. It cast a critical eye on the system. Marvin Miller, executive director of the Major League Baseball Players Association in 1981, helped finalize the agreement before retiring in 1982. Some felt the flawed system was Miller's departing gift to owners before leaving. For almost two decades, he made the players more powerful and rich, bringing them free agency and bargaining power. "Marvin Miller's final act was to devise the perfect system to get the owners mad at each other," Jerry Reinsdorf, former owner of the White Sox, said in 1984. Free agent compensation was doing just that.

As much as free agent compensation was drawing criticism, it was hard to villainize Oakland for doing their homework and using the system to their advantage. "The Yankees wish to make it clear that they find no fault with the management of the Oakland A's for exercising a different interpretation of the rules," Mel Southard, Yankees general counsel, said at the time. Oakland narrowed their list down to fifty players prior to circling over Belcher. If New York would have waited four more days to sign Belcher, he would have not been available for Oakland's taking. But the Yankees felt pressured to sign him fast to keep him from returning to Mount Vernon for his senior year and becoming ineligible. Sandy Alderson, the A's former general manager who orchestrated the move, remembered the context that brought him Belcher. "I think they just didn't understand the rules, and we quickly realized he was eligible," remembered Alderson. "The Yankees took him, signed him, and made this opportunity for us to take him. We communicated with the American League about taking Belcher, and they tried to talk us out of it. We ended up taking him. It became somewhat controversial."

Boldly and shrewdly taking Belcher from the Yankees set the tone for Alderson's tenure as a baseball executive. "That was Sandy's first claim to fame as someone who had just taken over our system," said Keith Lieppman, who began managing in the A's organization in 1980. "It was one of the first big moves he made, and it turned out to be a real good move for us." The rest of baseball took note of Oakland's studied and bold front office. They were a new breed. "Sandy was one of the guys who changed the face of how that office operated," said Belcher. "He wasn't just a former player sitting in a smoke-filled room with scouts. He had a law degree. He was a real analytical, well-read guy who was shrewd. Being the wise man he was, he noticed the No. 1 pick and the best prospect available was eligible for selection."

Back in New York, angry Yankees fans flooded the phone lines at Yankee Stadium to protest losing Belcher, prompting New York to file a formal protest with Lee MacPhail, director of baseball's Player Relations Committee, on February 14. They asserted they did not draft Belcher until January 17, four days after they filed their list of twenty-six protected players. Only players in the organization on the January 13 deadline should have been eligible for the compensation pool, they contended. The Yankees insisted they had no means of protecting Belcher.

MacPhail had ruled on New York's affairs the previous summer, when he handed down a highly publicized ruling against them. On July 24, 1983, home-plate umpire Tim McClelland erased Royals third baseman George Brett's two-run, game winning home run against New York at Yankee Stadium for allegedly having too much pine tar on the barrel of his bat. Kansas City filed a protest, and MacPhail overruled the umpires, crediting Brett with the home run and the Royals with the win for what came to be known as the Pine Tar Incident. MacPhail handed the Yankees more bad news in 1984. He tossed out the protest and ruled that Belcher belonged to Oakland. "The selection of Tim Belcher by Oakland shall stand, and the contract shall be assigned from Greensboro to the Oakland organization," MacPhail ruled.

Belcher remembered how the Yankees reacted when Oakland took him. "They were scrambling," he said. "They were calling me to find a way to disallow the pick. They hinted that if I petitioned to Major League Baseball that I had my heart set on playing in New York and that I grew up a Yankee fan, they would not approve the pick and make Oakland pick someone else. But at that point, Oakland seemed like a better opportunity for a young prospect. They offered me a quicker ascent to the big leagues than New York did at the time."

Steinbrenner was so angry, his front office was never the same. He stripped power from his executives and reassigned others. Cook's role as general manager was diminished. He was reassigned to scouting carrying a clipboard. Steinbrenner ordered him to remain in New York when the Yankees left for spring training. Bill Bergesch, formerly vice president of baseball operations, was transferred to baseball administration. Steinbrenner made Clyde King, a longtime close advisor, the new general manager. Bergesch and Cook left the organization by October. Cook was hired as the Montreal Expos' new general manager in September. Cincinnati hired Bergesch as new general manager in October.

Oakland invited Belcher to big league camp for spring training until Minor League camp opened at Scottsdale Community College in early March. Before arriving in Phoenix, Arizona, Belcher and Boras had flown to Oakland for a few days to meet A's executives. In Phoenix, Belcher shared lockers with Tom Romano in the spring. One of Belcher's highlights of being in big league camp with Oakland was meeting Joe Morgan, the A's forty-year-old second baseman. Belcher, a fan of Cincinnati's Big Red Machine teams of the 1970s, idolized Morgan, growing up in Ohio. But Belcher garnered his own attention, as the twice minted No. 1 pick swaggered into Phoenix for spring training on February 25. "He had the phenom label with the buzz of money when he got here," said Brad Fischer, Belcher's first manager in pro ball. He drew more attention than A's big leaguers. Belcher threw batting practice for ten minutes at Phoenix Municipal Stadium, Oakland's spring training headquarters. Everyone stopped and watched as he hit ninety-four miles an hour on the radar gun. He overmatched everyone. In Florida twenty-one-year-old Roger Clemens, another fireballing phenom in Boston's organization, was blowing batters away during the spring. Both phenoms were building the stage to become baseball's next version of Nolan Ryan and Seaver.

When spring training ended, Oakland sent Belcher north to Madison, Wisconsin, to begin his professional career playing for the Madison Muskies, one of the A's Single-A clubs, in the Midwest League. Many forecasted Belcher would dominate the Midwest League like Juan Nieves, an eighteen-year-old pitching prospect for the Milwaukee Brewers, did the prior season. One of the reasons Oakland favored sending Belcher to Madison as opposed to Single-A Modesto was they wanted him close to Wes Stock, the A's Minor League pitching coach. Stock planned on spending a great deal of time in Madison in 1984. While New York was on the hook for Belcher's $125,000 bonus, Oakland paid his salary—a little under $1,000 a month. Belcher was not short of confidence when he began his professional baseball journey. "I just want to be moved along as rapidly as I can," Belcher said in 1984. "If I'm ready to pitch in AA ball right now, that's where I want to be. If I'm ready for AA in July, that's where I want to be."

Belcher's wishes materialized as scheduled. After opening the season 6-0 for Madison, he posted a 9-4 record with a 3.57 earned run average in sixteen starts there. By July Oakland moved Belcher up to Double-A, and he played in the Eastern League for the Albany-Colonie A's. "I had a really good first year," said Belcher. "By the end of the year, I was in Double-A pitching in the Eastern League playoffs." Besides fighting through a rough four-game losing streak for Madison in June, Oakland was pleased with his development. During that stretch, Belcher learned to battle through his struggles on the mound. "Timmy had grit and was a battler," said Chip Conklin, Belcher's Minor League teammate. "You knew he was going to go out and battle for you."

The attention and pressure intensified for Belcher in Albany, the state capital of New York. The region was still reeling over the Yankees losing him. New York had filed another grievance and was awaiting a ruling from Bowie Kuhn, Major League Baseball's commissioner. Ben Bernard, owner of the Albany-Colonie club, recalled Belcher's East Coast arrival. "The New York media came with satellite trucks for his first outing. They all wanted to talk about this kid stolen from the Yankees."

In front of a hoard of media at Heritage Park, Albany-Colonie's ballpark, on July 14, Belcher was shelled early. He issued eight walks in one and two-thirds innings. He walked five straight batters at one point, taking the loss. "He started his first game in Albany by walking the first three guys and coughing up a home run," recalled Bernard. "It happened to him like two or three times in a row. It was the awfullest thing you could imagine for the kid. He was so upset, we flew his girlfriend in. I suggested we start him on the road to get the pressure off him. But he was a great young kid." Belcher was tough on himself and a ferocious competitor. "Tim was a little hot-headed," recalled Rick Stromer, a former Minor League teammate. "If he got rocked, he was not afraid to throw at the other team." Mike Ashman, another teammate in Albany in 1984, remembered pulling him aside on the bus on occasion to calm him. "He was really hard on himself," said Ashman. "He felt like he had to win every game and strike everyone out. He was so competitive." His nickname was soon "Hurricane" Belcher.

Belcher finished the season in Albany with a 3-4 record and a 3.33 earned run average. He admitted to being tired and losing zip on his fastball from pitching 153 innings at Madison and Albany combined in 1984, the most he ever pitched in a season. He battled wildness. "Tim had a strong arm, but he couldn't control the baseball sometimes," said Wayne Giddings, Belcher's teammate in Madison. "But Oakland was going to give him every opportunity to keep throwing until he found the strike zone."

Belcher finished the season strong, boasting an earned run average of 1.96 in his last four starts. He was pleased with his first year despite the chaos. "It was overwhelming at times," said Belcher. "I'm suddenly on a roster with a bunch of older, experienced guys in Albany. It was kind of a whirlwind for me. It was not long before I was on the campus of Mount Vernon Nazarene College pitching in the snow during the spring." Belcher reported to Arizona instructional league in Scottsdale after the season. Being invited to instructional league was a shot in the arm for him. It meant he was in Oakland's plans. Belcher finished his first year as a professional with a 12-8 record and 3.49 earned run average.

Bowie Kuhn finally ruled on New York's grievance and confirmed for good Belcher's fate in September. He ruled that Oakland's selection of Belcher was valid but awarded the Yankees a bonus pick at the conclusion of the first round of baseball's summer draft in 1985. "Oakland was not at fault in making the selection, but in my judgment, the Yankees certainly are deserving of some compensation themselves as a means of producing a fairer result," Kuhn said at the time. Players and owners eliminated free agent compensation in the next collective bargaining agreement in 1985.

With distractions behind him, Belcher zeroed in on his goal of making the big leagues by 1986.

Harvey Dorfman, Oakland's new psychologist, promoted a mental side of the game throughout the organization that behooved Belcher. "Harvey was very instrumental in helping him overcome some of the difficulties of learning how to play the game correctly and managing yourself," said Lieppman. "Tim was an outright very athletic kid—a great pitcher—and he benefited from this whole new style that we presented in our system when the new regime came in." After passing through the hands of two clubs since June, Belcher made himself at home in the A's organization. "Maybe the A's will be better for me," Belcher said in 1984. "I hope I made the right decision."

3

Albany Takeover

"We had already bounced around and had a championship-type season in Albany in 1984, but the Yankees decided to pursue Albany. The people there thought having a Yankee affiliate would be great for attendance, which certainly made sense. We were suddenly out in the cold looking for a spot."
—**SANDY ALDERSON**, A's former general manager, May 2021

With Detroit's Triple-A farm club relocating from Evansville to Nashville for the 1985 season, New York was forced to vacate Music City after five seasons and find a new Double-A home. There was a rumor the Yankees were transferring the farm club to Huntsville, Alabama, to stay in the Southern League under new ownership. The timing seemed perfect for the move. Joe W. Davis, Huntsville's mayor, was trying to bring professional baseball, and New York's popular farm club was available. Huntsville's lack of a suitable stadium for Minor League Baseball had always kept the city from serious talks to land a team, but Davis was serious about building one. As New York packed their bags in Nashville, George Steinbrenner, the Yankees' brazen owner, harbored no resentment to Larry Schmittou or Nashville for having to leave. Despite the inconvenience, he understood the move. "They have a sound program, and they have a chance to move ahead," Steinbrenner said in 1984. "We had a great relationship with Larry Schmittou and the fine people there and wish them nothing but the best." The Yankees' mystique in Nashville was going to be a hard act to follow. They were the model club and class of the Southern League since 1980, but Schmittou's plan was wider and deeper. Bringing Triple-A baseball to Nashville, he thought, would bring them a step closer to landing a Major League franchise.

It wasn't long before New York found a new Double-A home. Back east, Billy Martin, an advisor for the Yankees in 1984, was pulling strings behind the scenes to bring the farm club to New York, closer to home. And Albany, New York, a city part of the Eastern League, was becoming available. Oakland had planted a Double-A club in Albany in 1983, but their contract with Ben Bernard, owner of the Albany-Colonie A's, was expiring after the 1984 season. Bernard, a Yankees enthusiast, met Martin through Pete Whisenant, Albany-Colonie's manager in 1983. Whisenant was Martin's buddy and former teammate. When Martin was managing in Oakland, he hired Whisenant to work with A's farmhands. In 1982 Whisenant led the Single-A Modesto A's to a California League championship and was crowned the league's Manager of the Year before promoting to manage Albany in 1983. Martin arranged for Bernard to meet Yankees officials to discuss a move to Albany for the 1985 season. "The Yankees wanted in there really bad," recalled Keith Lieppman, who managed Albany-Colonie in 1983–84.

The Albany alliance made perfect sense for Bernard and New York. Landing the Yankees would be a big splash and validate his decision to bring Minor League Baseball back to the city in 1983. Bernard was making all the right moves. He had monitored the baseball awakenings happening in other towns like Louisville and Nashville and wanted the Capital Region to experience the same excitement. "I was always watching everything happening in the Minor Leagues, especially in those cities," said Bernard. "I was hoping we could learn from them, and that Albany could be a great destination for Minor League Baseball."

Bernard was a rising star in the industry. In his twenties, he had already built a strong name for himself in the Eastern League. Before moving a new franchise to Albany in 1983, Bernard was general manager of the Glens Falls White Sox, Chicago's Double-A affiliate in New York. He was the league's executive of the year in 1982 before resigning. The twenty-seven-year-old purchased the fledgling West Haven club from David Goldstein that year for $100,000 and moved the franchise to Albany for the 1983 season. Despite winning the Eastern League championship in 1982, West Haven drew only fifty-one thousand fans at Quigley Stadium. A frustrated Goldstein was ready to sell, and Bernard brought a franchise to Albany for the first time since the Albany Senators, a Kansas City A's affiliate, were contracted in 1959.

Bernard's priority in Albany was to build a new ballpark, and he did. By July 1983 Heritage Park, a $1.5 million facility in the town of Colonie, an Albany suburb, was built. Albany played at fifty-year-old Bleecker Stadium, a hitter-friendly, glorified high school bandbox, until Heritage Park was ready in the summer. Given that five-thousand-seat Heritage Park, financed by Albany County and the town of Colonie, was now technically in Colonie, the club was called the Albany-Colonie A's instead of Albany A's when it opened for play.

Bernard, after purchasing the West Haven franchise, inherited a working agreement with Oakland that expired after the 1984 season, so A's farmhands came with him to Albany. Both sides were comfortable with the Albany partnership. "The facility was certainly better than what we had in West Haven and the owners were great to work with," recalled Walt Jocketty, the A's farm director at the time. Oakland emphasized player development and invested a lot of money in their farm system ever since Walter A. Haas Jr. purchased the franchise from Charlie Finley in 1980. By 1982 all six of the A's farm clubs reached the postseason and boasted an overall winning percentage of .635, the highest of any organization.

In 1983 Albany-Colonie was an older club composed of championship talent under manager Whisenant. Oakland fed Albany-Colonie with players from their winning Single-A clubs in Madison, Wisconsin, and Modesto, California. While the Modesto A's, considered a higher brand of Single-A, won the California League championship in 1982, the Madison Muskies, led by manager Brad Fischer, were also winning in the Midwest League and reached the postseason. Oakland also supplied Albany-Colonie with players from West Haven, the 1982 Eastern League champions. Steve Kiefer, once compared by A's director of scouting Dick Wiencek to a "skinny Robin Yount," manned shortstop.

Mark Ferguson, Modesto's top pitcher who posted a 17-6 record with an earned run average of 1.77 in 1982, joined Albany's staff. Oakland's top picks in 1982, Steve Ontiveros, a right-handed pitcher from the University of Michigan and Phil Stephenson, a first baseman from Wichita State, opened the season in Albany.

The return of pro baseball brought excitement to the area, and dozens of Albany players eventually reached the Major Leagues. "We drew good with Oakland for two years in a row with a small ballpark that held only six thousand people," said Bernard. "But we had some huge standing-room-only crowds." But even with the club pushing the needle in Albany, Oakland was not Bernard's first choice. Oakland accompanied the West Haven purchase. He was a self-proclaimed fan of the Yankees, and Oakland knew they were in Yankees country.

Bernard, owner and general manager, had a reputation for being a clever promoter who knew how to attract fans. On September 3, 1983, Bernard was behind Mike Ashman becoming the first player ever to play all ten positions in the season finale game against the Nashua Angels. He felt that Ashman's unusual, record-breaking feat at Heritage Park would attract fans. Bernard first received the go-ahead from Jocketty before promoting the stunt in advance. Ashman, a versatile utility player, joked with Bernard that he wanted special compensation for going through with it, specifically fifty cents for every beer sold during the game. Bernard laughed it off and declined. "Walt approved Bernard's idea and we did it," recalled Ashman. "Ben promoted it and we had a fun night. He knew what he was doing. We had a big crowd." Only two other Major Leaguers, Bert Campaneris in 1965 and Cesar Tover in 1968, had played all nine positions. "Even if it was a publicity stunt, it was quite an achievement," Jocketty said at the time. "Not everybody is that versatile."

Bernard's bag of tricks didn't bring many wins on the field, however. Albany-Colonie finished in fifth place in the eight-team Eastern League in 1983, with a record of 63-73, thirty-one games behind the first place Reading Phillies, who were later eliminated in the playoffs. The club's struggle and lack of overall direction reached a point that

Oakland made a managerial change midseason. The A's fired Whisenant during a five-game winning streak in July. But Albany-Colonie's losing record wasn't the only cause for Whisenant's dismissal. His emphasis on winning clashed with Oakland's focus on player development. Player development was secondary to him, the organization felt. There were also reports that during pregame workouts, Whisenant, fifty-three, completed lineups on a napkin from a local bar and sent it to the pitching coach to post. "He was late to the ballpark a few times, but he was a very good manager to play for and knew baseball," said Charlie O'Brien, the club's catcher and former Major Leaguer.

Ray Alonzo, an offensive sparkplug for the club in 1983, told reporters about some dysfunction in Albany when he rejoined Madison in August that season. "These guys should have seen the mess at Albany," he said in 1983. "They were bringing in people, sending them out. They were firing coaches. They didn't know if they were winning or losing. There aren't many happy players in Albany." Oakland replaced Whisenant with thirty-four-year-old Keith Lieppman, manager of their Pioneer League club in Idaho Falls, Idaho. Lieppman was a promising manager working his way up in the organization. "We had a few prospects that we didn't feel were being developed properly down there and I was sent to fire Pete and introduce Keith," said Jocketty. "To get the club's development back on track, we put together a group of instructors to run a minicamp with workouts every morning. Keith was the perfect choice to take over the team as his career path is well documented."

Sandy Alderson, the A's former vice president of baseball operations, remembered Lieppman's rise in the organization. "Keith started in the organization as a player," said Alderson. "He transitioned to coaching and made his way up the chain. He even predated Billy Martin in Oakland." Whisenant, after being fired, hinted that his friendship with Martin led to his dismissal. "I'm one of Billy's boys," he said. "I'm not the iced tea drinker some of those other guys are. Maybe they're trying to weed out Billy Martin's beer drinkers."

Alderson said that when Oakland fired Martin after the 1982 season, a lot of Billy's hires, mostly friends, stayed with the organization. Some lasted longer than others. Martin had brought friends in as scouts, coaches, managers, special instructors, broadcasters, and in several other capacities. But now they were there without Martin's juice. Because Martin had full autonomy as manager and director of player development for the A's, his departure meant Oakland's front office needed to develop their own identity and brand for success. Martin rescued the dying A's franchise on the verge of relocation when he came over in 1980.

"Billy Ball" rocked Oakland and was the baseball show in the Bay Area for three years, shattering the A's all-time season attendance record by 1982. He made the A's into one of America's most popular sports franchises. It was Billy's world, and the A's and the city gave him the keys to the kingdom. Alderson; Roy Eisenhardt, the club's president; and Wally Haas, vice president and son of owner Walter A. Haas Jr., joined along for the ride, but they knew they needed to come up with their own plan with "Billy Ball" behind them. "Billy had been very successful in leading the A's to the playoffs in 1981, but his style was a very different approach to the game," said Alderson. "It was an old school approach that Billy, his coaching staff, and the people he put in place in the Minor League system represented. All of them were basically his friends. But at the time, he was the only one in the organization that had any baseball experience aside from the people he brought in. When Billy left, we didn't have much infrastructure and realized we needed to have sort of a broader representation of the baseball industry, so we listened to people with different viewpoints and perspectives. It was also about the time analytics was emerging as a potential means for evaluating players."

Oakland meant business about developing players. If coaches or managers, including Martin's hires, were not endorsing that philosophy in the Minor Leagues, they were dismissed. The A's refused to sacrifice development for wins. Alderson made sure of that. Some of them adjusted and some did not. "When Sandy came in, he wanted to move people that weren't ready to get on board with the new way things were being done," recalled Lieppman. "The people who didn't want to get on board, got fired. If you weren't willing to follow what they wanted to do, they gave you a short leash, and if you didn't respond, they went with younger guys like me." And young guys like Lieppman; Fischer, twenty-six; and Grady Fuson, twenty-seven, an area scout and A's Minor League summer coach, took the torch. "Up until that 1984 season, our Minor Leagues were in shambles a little bit," recalled Lieppman.

Oakland kept building. They hired the innovative, forty-five-year-old Karl Kuehl, former manager of the Montreal Expos in 1976 and third base coach for the Minnesota Twins since 1977, as a roving Minor League instructor in the spring. Kuehl brought with him a psychological approach—a mental awareness of the game—that he stressed to players. Kuehl also brought his friend, Harvey Dorfman, a sports psychologist from Manchester, Vermont, to counsel players on any matters weighing on them on and off the field. Dorfman, a former high school and college pitcher, studied psychology in college and was a former baseball columnist. The forty-eight-year-old was an English teacher at Burr and Burton Seminary. Dorfman focused on the Minor Leagues and started working with Albany players. He was baseball's first fulltime counselor, and he established a niche. "This kind of thing is not new to sports—it's just new to baseball," Dorfman said in 1984.

He suited up and met with players in the outfield, in the dugout, clubhouse, and behind the batting cage before games. He was available to counsel them on the pressures of the Minor Leagues and the psychology of baseball. He represented a nonthreatening figure to them. Coaches recommended players to meet with Dorfman, and they took advantage of him being around. "It was one of the greatest moves in baseball," said Greg Cadaret, a former Major Leaguer who pitched in the A's system for five seasons. "He ended up being very important in my career. I was a mess. The best thing Karl ever did was bring him in."

Ray Thoma, shortstop for Albany-Colonie in 1984, said Dorfman's presence in baseball was trailblazing. More focus was being placed on the mental side of the game. "That was the precursor to how involved sports psychology would be in the game today," Thoma said. "That was the start of baseball becoming a mental game." Thoma was once mired in a 0-for-55 slump, and someone made him Dorfman's first project. Thoma wasn't looking foolish at the plate. He was driving balls that fielders made plays on. But the hitless streak frustrated the twenty-two-year-old. Tension was building inside of him from the pressure. He threw Dorfman off when the psychologist introduced himself. "I just started twitching in front of him," Thoma chuckled. "As he looked at me, I told him I was having a hard time because I couldn't stop twitching and it disturbed me while I was at the plate. We were just messing with him." Dorfman turned to Kuehl: "What the fuck is going on here?" he asked. Thoma kept making outs. When Dorfman caught Thoma's attention returning to the dugout after making another out, his advice was simple: keep swinging the bat. "Fuck you, Harvey . . . I'm so tired of hearing your shit," Thoma barked at him. But Thoma kept swinging, and two days later, his drives started dropping for hits. He broke out of the slump. Thoma realized that Dorfman was onto something. "Having a mental coach was different," Thoma said.

By August 1983 Oakland made Kuehl the director of player development. A new sheriff was in town and his message was clear: "Winning ballgames in the Minors is not the priority," Kuehl said in 1983. "We develop to win, not win to develop." Kuehl had recently banned alcohol from the clubhouse and team bus. "When Karl took over, it was his way or the highway," remembered Fischer. "He was going to change the culture that existed there. He changed everything and set us all on a good path." Kuehl was a major part of Oakland's future success, according to Alderson.

It was a subculture of hard drinking and edgy, barroom behavior the conservative A's front office wanted to distance themselves from. Steve Kiefer, shortstop for Albany in 1983, described the disconnect between Oakland's new emphasis on development and the win-immediately mentality. With Martin no longer being the focal point of the franchise, Oakland toned down the emphasis and gambling style urgency to win. "A lot of the people Billy brought over had a different mentality, so there was a clash," said Kiefer. "When Billy was there, they really didn't work on the Minor League system. They would acquire people with a win-at-all-cost mentality. Once he left, Oakland's mentality was now to build the organization and develop players for the big leagues." Oakland was not finished. Ed Nottle—manager for Triple-A Tacoma and another one of Martin's 1980 hires—got the ax after the 1984 season. "Ed was not going to adapt to anybody else's way of doing things," recalled Fischer. "He wanted to do his own thing. There was friction. There was a difference in philosophy."

Oakland was cleaning house and shaking up their farm system. In addition to making Kuehl in charge of player development during the shakeup, Alderson, formerly vice president and general counsel, was promoted to vice president of baseball operations, and Dick Wiencek became director of scouting. Wiencek and Jocketty were responsible for populating the farm clubs. At the big league level, Oakland handed rookie manager Steve Boros, forty-seven, a contract extension for another year despite a losing record of 74-88 and fourth place finish in the American League West.

In 1983 Oakland's farm system didn't have the winning touch it had in 1982. The six clubs combined for a .509 winning percentage. Only Oakland's short-season, Single-A club in Medford, Oregon, managed by Dennis Rogers, won a championship in the Northwest League by virtue of a 50-18 record. "Our philosophy is to win and develop," Jocketty said at the time. "Last year we won, this year we developed." Development was the theme for the entire organization in 1983.

Back in Albany, despite Whisenant's dismissal and a losing season, the major story was the return of professional baseball in a new stadium. "It was a breath of fresh air," remembered Donald Moore, an A's fan who watched Albany-Colonie play. "The people supported the club. It was something new." Mike Ashman remembered the excitement that came with a new ballpark. "Once they opened up the new park, we had a blast," said Ashman. "We had some big crowds with a lot of energy. It was a fun place to play, and the area enjoyed the team." While the Buffalo Bisons led the league with a season attendance of 200,531, Albany-Colonie was right behind them, drawing 200,126 fans combined in both ballparks. The Glens Falls White Sox played only fifty miles away from Albany, sparking a rivalry. They played for the Mayor's Trophy over sixteen games during the season.

On the field, A's farmhands in Albany made their mark. Mike Warren, who posted a 6-2 record with a 3.25 earned run average for Albany-Colonie in 1983, tossed a no-hitter later that season for parent club Oakland on September 29 against Tony La Russa's White Sox. Ontiveros anchored the rotation with an 8-4 record and 3.75 earned run average. The club strutted power on the infield. Stephenson; Kiefer, the shortstop; and Tim Pyznarski, at third, clubbed a combined sixty-seven homers. Outfielder Tom Romano, meanwhile, purchased from the Utica Blue Sox in 1981, amassed twenty-four. Pyznarski was Oakland's first-round pick, and fifteenth overall, in the June Amateur Draft in 1981. Future Major Leaguers O'Brien, Ontiveros, Warren, Pyznarski, Stephenson, Romano, Kiefer, Luis Quinones, Mike Gallego, and Rich Wortham played for Albany-Colonie in 1983. Pitcher Ken Kravec had played for the White Sox and Chicago Cubs before joining Albany-Colonie that season.

Lieppman turned Albany-Colonie around in 1984. He led the club to the Eastern League division title with a record of 81-57 before being eliminated by the Vermont Reds in the playoffs. "Keith did a good job in Albany," said Fischer. "He's a tremendous baseball guy. He did a great job relating to the players and earned the opportunity to go to Triple-A the following season."

The 1984 club was composed mostly of players from Modesto and sprinkled with some from Madison. Belcher, who posted a dazzling record of 9-4 with a 3.57 earned run average for Madison, was promoted to Albany by July. In contrast to 1983, the club lacked power. No Albany player reached double digits in homers that season. They drew 199,534 at Heritage Park, and Lieppman was named Eastern League Manager of the Year. "We had a strong team," remembered Thoma, "but playing in the Eastern League was so different from other leagues. There were some empty stadiums, and bad weather affected more games than any league I ever played in. I did enjoy seeing the historic parks of the league." The club held a split-squad scrimmage at Buffalo's War

Memorial Stadium, where the 1984 baseball classic *The Natural* was filmed. Visiting The Anchor Bar, the birthplace of Buffalo wings, was another fun experience for A's farmhands in Albany.

But the Yankees came on the scene shortly after Schmittou decided to elevate Nashville to Triple-A in July 1984. Oakland's stay in Albany was short-lived. The A's contract with Bernard expired after the 1984 season, and they knew they were sitting ducks in Yankees territory. Jocketty knew Bernard preferred an East Coast team. "Things started developing with New York coming out of Nashville," Bernard said. After being seduced by the Yankees, Bernard inked a two-year working agreement with them on September 26, 1984. "We had a championship-type season in Albany in 1984, but the Yankees decided to pursue Albany," said Alderson. "The people there thought having a Yankee affiliate would be great for attendance, which certainly made sense. We were suddenly out in the cold looking for a spot." Albany now belonged to the Yankees to the delight of Bernard, who idolized owner George Steinbrenner and was a disciple of the Yankees way. Partnering with New York meant he was connected to Steinbrenner. "Growing up being aggressive in the business, I always felt like Steinbrenner was my boss," said Bernard. Plus, Albany was only a two-hour drive from Yankee Stadium, thousands of miles closer than Nashville was. "The owners wanted to emulate the Yankee style at the time, and the Yankees anticipated a nice, close relationship with them," said Lieppman. "It made sense for both parties." Bernard jumped on the opportunity. "Billy got me to the right people, and the next thing I know, they talked to me about a player development contract," recalled Bernard. "Being in Yankee territory, I'd be a fool to turn them down, especially being the capitol of New York. Bringing the Yankees in really made the franchise take off."

As the Yankees vacated Nashville, the move bumped the A's from Albany and the Eastern League. "We enjoyed Albany, but the Yankees came and took over the franchise," remembered Jocketty, an executive advisor for the Cincinnati Reds today. "They knew they would draw better as a Yankee affiliate over a West Coast team. It was Yankee territory. We weren't happy about it, but we understood their motivation." Bernard broke the news to Jocketty over dinner, and Oakland tried to change his mind. They offered him a Major League exhibition game to stay in Albany, but Bernard made up his mind. "Even though I certainly had some good friends with the A's, I opted to go with the Yankees," said Bernard. "I felt bad. Oakland was great. They sent Ron Schueler and Fred "Chicken" Stanley from the front office to talk to me because I knew them. But I told them I had to do this because the whole area will go crazy. It was a win-win for us."

Bernard noted that after the Yankees came in 1985, the NAPBL allowed the club to wear real Yankees uniforms because they were in the state capital. City initials were not required on Albany's uniforms. "Local politicians were a little upset at me, but I asked them, if they bought a McDonald's franchise, would they tear down the golden arches," said Bernard. "Coming to the ballpark seeing Yankee uniforms was a big deal for kids in those days."

Some speculated New York's capture of Albany was payback to Oakland for scooping Belcher from them in the free agent compensation pool in February. While Nashville and Albany anticipated a new parade of baseball coming in 1985, Oakland was left out in the cold. With Albany now behind them, Jocketty needed to hustle and find a new home for the farm club, their sixth Double-A home since 1976. "I was responsible for finding a new Double-A affiliate," recalled Jocketty. Oakland was forced into playing musical chairs and needed to find a seat. Fast.

4

Rocket City

"We had a beautiful downtown area but didn't have a big event to bring us together. We hosted civic center concerts but adding baseball to what we already had boosted the quality of life for the whole community. The magic of it was having local ownership. It gave us that local flavor. We sat there, talked, and watched baseball."—**TOMMY BATTLE**, mayor, Huntsville, 2021

July 1984: Joe W. Davis, the sixty-five-year-old mayor of Huntsville since 1968, was at the forefront of transforming the city into a technology superpower. Many considered the innovative mayor a city father. Davis, a former teacher and real estate specialist, served as mayor for twenty years—five four-year terms of visionary leadership. Before serving as mayor, he was a special assistant to Glenn Hearn, who held the seat previously. Davis made Huntsville into California's version of Silicon Valley, a global hotbed known for innovation and trend-setting technology in the Bay Area. He recruited high-tech industries to settle in Huntsville when space cutbacks leveled the economy in the early 1970s. Many wondered how the end of the Apollo program would impact the once booming economy. In fact, a United Press International article published on October 24, 1968, conveyed the worry: "The city still advertises itself as the 'space capital of the world.' But a nagging doubt persists that the end of the Apollo program may signal the death-knell of this city."

The city's new residents who came for work were critical in helping the economy survive and thrive. Huntsville added forty-five thousand new industrial jobs under the spell of Davis. As many settled in Huntsville for high-tech jobs, the population soared to more than 160,000. Davis was named the country's top mayor in 1975. "He was an excellent mayor and a forward thinker," recalled John Pruett.

The city's technology renaissance in the 1970s lured a new, sophisticated, highly educated, affluent population from all over the world. The old, tired, rural cotton town of thirteen thousand in 1940 now had a cosmopolitan vibe in contrast to other cities in Alabama. Because Alabama was not known for technology, Huntsville's high-tech boom was largely unnoticed. The city transformed into a hotbed for research and development filled with highly educated engineers and scientists. Huntsville was establishing an image independent of Alabama tradition and leaving behind agricultural dependency from decades earlier.

The industrial days of coal and cotton in Huntsville were over. Cotton mills were the heart and soul of the city's economy beginning in the late nineteenth century. The mills transformed cotton into fibers and yarns for the town's emerging textile industry. Huntsville's textile industry became one of the South's most lucrative industries and put the city on the map. But Huntsville's image dramatically changed shortly after World War II. The city once dubbed the "watercress capital of the world" became a space-age town. The face of Huntsville's new look was Wernher von Braun, one of over one hundred German-born aerospace engineers designing missiles at Peenemunde Army Research Center in Germany that American forces brought to the United States in 1945 as the war ended in Europe. While von Braun, the thirty-three-year-old chief architect, had designed v-2 rockets for Adolf Hitler during the war, his primary ambition was to master rocketry. The United States insisted on interrogating von Braun, one of Germany's top scientists and engineers. The expectation for von Braun was to use the rocketry intelligence he championed in Germany to advance the United States. Because von Braun was considered too valuable, he was not prosecuted for his alliance with the Nazi regime and German war effort. By 1950 von Braun and the other German engineers were deployed in Huntsville to develop rockets and missiles for the U.S. Army—ones capable of carrying nuclear warheads. He changed Huntsville forever when he arrived. Von Braun hastened the dawn of the space age and revolutionized the art of warfare through rocketry. "When he moved here, it changed everything," said Rick Davis, former radio voice of the Huntsville Stars. "Huntsville was literally a tiny cotton town in North Alabama."

The army juiced the small farm town with people, equipment, and money. In 1958 the United States established NASA, the National Aeronautics and Space Administration, and opened the George C. Marshall Space Flight Center in Huntsville in 1960 as a successor to the Redstone Arsenal, where most of the U.S. Army's early missile initiatives were carried out. The space center became NASA's largest research center and focused on developing rockets for orbit. Von Braun was tapped the center's first director. Fueled by the space race with the Soviet Union, President John F. Kennedy announced, in 1961 to a joint session in Congress, a plan to land an American on the moon "before this decade is out."

The space race established a new platform for von Braun and offered him an opportunity to advance his obsession of space travel. He seized the moment. The mission of beating the Soviet Union to the moon was intense. Von Braun and his team developed and built the Saturn V, the world's largest rocket. The space marvel was three thousand tons and thirty-six stories, generating 7.5 million pounds of thrust in its first stage. The forty-one-engine rocket was designed, built, and tested at Marshall Space Flight Center in Huntsville. Kennedy was not around for the moon-landing as he was assassinated on November 22, 1963, in Dallas, Texas. But on July 16, 1969, *Apollo 11* was launched from John F. Kennedy Space Center, Cape Kennedy. An audience of 650 million watched the liftoff on television, and man landed on the moon on July 20. Mission accomplished.

Von Braun's fame grew around the world after *Apollo 11*. The charismatic space mogul established himself as an ambassador for space exploration and built a rocket empire in Huntsville. He was charming and insisted on perfection. Von Braun not only possessed the technical prowess of building a moon machine, but he also knew how to sell it. He brought millions in funding to the space program, making Huntsville the economic pillar of Alabama. Von Braun was a consultant for Walt Disney, and Disney came to Huntsville on many occasions to meet with him. Von Braun was a renaissance man who had a curiosity about everything around him. "He was the superstar of space of his day," Bob Ward, biographer of the legendary von Braun, said in 2013. "He had a passion for life, rocketry, and space exploration, and it showed through all of his work and communications." He popularized the notion of space travel. Von Braun—ambitious about space exploration since childhood—became the godfather of the booming space program.

Economy in Huntsville was budding with new laboratories and test facilities. "Von Braun's arrival changed everything," said Rick Davis. "By 1969 we had a man on the moon. That's how Huntsville's technology sector began to grow. Witnessing a tiny cotton town grow up to be a haven for rocket development was neat."

Space and rockets became the center of major innovation projects and created more interest in the area. New challenges in technology birthed new industries—spinoffs from existing companies. There was a new sense of purpose for the town. Huntsville had moon fever. Von Braun's research was expensive. Apollo was a $25 billion investment and lured skeptics. Some critics in Huntsville, for example, felt that funding for the space programs should be invested in the cotton industry instead. Other skeptics were uncomfortable about his space agenda. One Huntsville woman once told him to quit testing God with his space plans for humans. "Stay at home and watch television like the Lord intended people to do," she explained to him. But von Braun and NASA had positioned themselves for more manned moon landings, and by 1969 only one cotton mill was left in Huntsville. The space program launched Huntsville into prosperity.

The Apollo program was a victim of its own success, however, and one moon landing after another was a little redundant, some felt. The necessity of the space program diminished in the eyes of politicians once Apollo succeeded, and crewed landings ended by 1972. Citing limited public interest in *Apollo 12*, the *New York Times* concluded in 1969 that a collective sense of anticlimax was "perhaps predictable considering the intense national emotion spent on the first moon landing four months ago." Fueled by America's obsession to beat the Soviet Union to the moon, some critics insisted *Apollo 11* was motivated by ego, prestige, and bragging rights, not scientific goals.

Funding for Apollo fell by nearly 50 percent, and America's priorities shifted. President Richard Nixon, and the American public increasingly turned their backs on the moon, and the Apollo program suffered deep budget cuts. Plus, tensions between Russia and the United States that sparked a space rivalry were easing. Public and Congress support was eroding. The closure of the Apollo program crippled Huntsville's economy in the early 1970s, and NASA employment in Huntsville declined. From a peak of 7,000 employees in the late 1960s, NASA's numbers dropped to 3,300 in the late 1970s. Once NASA took a fall, so did jobs and the economy. Many of Huntsville's private high-tech companies began layoffs. The "space bust" sent thousands of now unemployed, highly skilled engineers packing. "When the last two or three Apollo launches were canceled because of budget cutbacks, IBM shut its doors the next day and three to four thousand people left," said Davis.

But the resurgence of NASA-related activities and the space shuttle ultimately helped revive the area. Mayor Davis aggressively recruited companies to Rocket City to make up for the city's dramatic loss of space funding. Engineers came from all over the United States to populate Huntsville for work. Corporate companies like Xerox, Chrysler, TRW, Northrop, Lockheed, and Boeing created a new Huntsville.

Davis's recruitment efforts facing the roller coaster of space funding were critical to sustain the economy. By 1984 Huntsville was the home of 180 high-tech companies and became the major high-tech mecca of the South. If Alabama landed a supercomputer, Huntsville was the leading location to host it. "More than any of the other examined cities, Huntsville has its fortunes tied to the national demand for products that utilize the skills of high-tech manpower," Ernst Goss, an Alabama professor, said in 1985. Only Silicon Valley had a higher concentration of high-tech workers than Huntsville. Engineers, computer scientists, physicists, programmers, and science technicians settling in the city were highly educated and paid well, earning more than other high-tech employees around the country. They developed computers, calculators, ignition systems for cars, and military hardware. High-tech companies brought Huntsville $2 to $3 billion per year. Madison County boasted the lowest unemployment in the state, the highest per capita income, and the highest educational level. Some economists forecasted that President Ronald Reagan's Strategic Defense Initiative, widely known as Star Wars, would lure more million-dollar government contracts to Huntsville.

Rick Davis said the succinct partnership in Huntsville among government officials, local businesses, and the community made the city attractive. "Being in Huntsville is almost like a fairytale existence and the people here see the advantages of working together," he said. "Government and business are often in lockstep here, unlike other communities. If you wish for it, it will materialize here most of the time. It's not by accident so many good things have happened here. It's by design."

But as Huntsville became a mecca for technology and grew in population and prosperity, it lacked a social outlet to bring the community together. "We had a beautiful downtown area but didn't have a big event to bring us together," recalled Tommy Battle. While the city hosted concerts that lured crowds at local civic centers, a spark to pull families together was missing. "Back then, there really wasn't much in Huntsville other than the space and rocket center," said Cynthia Giles, a longtime Huntsville resident and former director of ticket sales for the Stars. The University of Alabama and Auburn University football pulled the most interest from the sports world. College football was king.

During the summer of 1984, Huntsville was presented with a chance to bring family entertainment in the form of a professional sports club to fill the void. Larry Schmittou had purchased the Triple-A Evansville Triplets in July and was moving the American Association franchise to

Nashville. Nashville's new Triple-A club continued under the "Nash-ville Sounds" name. Schmittou, though, needed a home to move his existing Southern League franchise in Nashville. Since 1978 he made the Double-A franchise a premier Minor League attraction. Schmittou's purchase of the Evansville club ultimately opened the door for Huntsville to land a team. He started discussions with Mayor Davis about bringing the franchise to Rocket City. The community-minded Davis was a sports fan and entertained the idea. "Davis was a very personable guy, so when Schmittou approached him, he was very enthusiastic and all for it," said John Pruett, who covered the move for the *Huntsville Times*. "Had he not been enthusiastic, I don't think Schmittou would have pursued it any further. Between the two of them, they worked it out."

The city had hosted pro baseball in the past—fifty-five years earlier, in 1930. The Class D Huntsville Springers played in the Georgia-Alabama League before the Great Depression wiped out the team and league. "The city had a Class D team in the early 1930s, so it had essentially been without professional baseball," the late Bob Mayes said in 2007. "Before the Space Age explosion, Huntsville was a very small town."

Almost three decades before the Springers were born, Huntsville fielded a club in the four-city Tennessee-Alabama League, in 1903, and won the pennant in the one-month season. The league was not affil-iated with any Major League clubs. The TAL increased to eight teams in 1904 but dropped to six by July that season. The club and league folded after the season. After having a club in the Tri-State League in 1905, the Huntsville Westerns, renamed the Mountaineers a year later, joined the Southeastern League in 1911 before moving to Talladega the following season. The city was without a club until the Springers arrived and played in the Georgia-Alabama League.

Semipro, mill-sponsored baseball was the major entertainment of the spring and summer in the 1930s. Playing or watching, baseball was a diversion in Huntsville during hard times. Americans had fallen in love with the sport. Huntsvillians embraced community baseball. Before the invention of the television and drive-ins, entertainment options were few and watching a game fit the bill. Some mill players were talented enough to be Major Leaguers, some historians insisted. The cotton mill leagues fizzled at the start of World War II, and labor union strife contributed to the decline. Major mills had shut down shortly after the war, and some wondered if mill baseball would return. But amateur teams resurfaced. The late Hub Myhand and Jim Talley were key figures of the era. While Myhand was considered Huntsville's "Mr. Baseball" before the war, Talley kept the baseball scene alive after. The Huntsville Manufacturing team had a run in the late 1940s before folding in 1955. In 1950 the Huntsville Boosters, playing at Optimist Park, became the first team to represent the city at the National Baseball Congress World Series in Wichita, Kansas. The Boosters folded in 1953 and the Parkers became Huntsville's team. As the Boosters, Parkers, and Merchants represented the city in the 1950s, Talley formed the Huntsville Independents in 1965. The Independents became one of Alabama's top amateur teams over the next decade.

During the mill-team era, a lot of great players passed through when they moved around the South. "Several famous players, including Babe Ruth and Ty Cobb, regularly came through Huntsville on their way back from spring training in Florida," Pruett said. "Huntsville was always a good baseball town because of the mill teams. We had several cotton mills and they all brought good players and hired them to play on their teams. In the 1930s and '40s, mill baseball was really big in Huntsville." The closing of the mills eventually ended the mill leagues.

Mayor Davis loved the idea of reviving baseball in Huntsville and bringing a new club to town, but the city did not have a big enough stadium to accommodate Double-A baseball. Schmittou assured Davis that if he built a ballpark in Huntsville, he would move the franchise there. Davis started building momentum by meeting with architects for a new city-funded stadium. Davis had a way of moving in a room of vultures and seeing new initiatives approved and labor disputes settled. It was hard to bet against the progressive World War II veteran. He made things happen. Davis anticipated what life baseball could bring to the city. "He saw bringing baseball as a part of our economic development and quality of life," said Tommy Battle. "Quite frankly, he liked baseball, too. It was a passion for him." Schmittou sensed Davis's excitement to bring baseball to engage the community. "He wanted it there very much and the city was hungry for an outlet to unite the community," Schmittou recalled. Pro baseball would be new entertainment for Huntsville, a city known for hunting down new industries.

According to Mayes, there were whispers of baseball returning to Huntsville before, but the idea never gained any significant momentum. In the early 1970s, the late Glenn Wallace, who later served as director of Huntsville Parks and Recreation for over a decade, had for years promoted a new multiuse stadium that would accommodate professional baseball, high school and college sports, and outdoor concerts. The Huntsville-born Wallace played locally at Butler High and starred as a pitcher for Mississippi State University in the late 1960s. He also pitched for the Huntsville Independents, a talented team that captured the Alabama state championship in 1966. Wallace was rooted in Huntsville.

The Milwaukee Braves drafted him out of high school in the fortieth round in 1965, and, in 1968, the Baltimore Orioles selected him from college in the forty-eighth round. Wallace never played in the Majors, but he started a tireless push to bring professional baseball to Huntsville. "He floated the idea of bringing baseball to Huntsville, but it never gained any support," the late Mayes once said. Wallace often served as a liaison between the city, league, and owner. Mayes wrote about Wallace's influence in the *Huntsville Times* in 1985: "But you've got to understand that without the dedication and the efforts of this man, there would be no Minor League Baseball team in Huntsville this summer and no state-of-the-art stadium for the city to enjoy," Mayes wrote.

Huntsville had been on Schmittou's radar for some time. In the early 1980s, he considered moving his Nashville hockey team, the South Stars, there during a spat with the city's Metro Council. He had ownership ties to five highly successful Minor League clubs. He was eyeing Huntsville as a destination to bring a Single-A franchise in 1982.

"I would like to see Minor League Baseball in Huntsville," Schmittou said in 1982. "I believe Huntsville could support a Class-A team and I believe Huntsville will get a team sometime in the near future. I've played several games in Huntsville and I know the city would support such a team." That year, Schmittou told Davis and Wallace that Huntsville needed a stadium with a seating capacity of at least five thousand to accommodate a club. Schmittou insisted that Minor League Baseball would bring 125 new jobs to Huntsville and $2 million back into the economy. The city drew up stadium plans in 1980 for a proposed multipurpose stadium with AstroTurf and a capacity of 9,500 that would cost $2.3 million. But the plans never materialized. "I would like to see the city get a professional baseball team," Davis said in 1982. "We have talked to the city council before about building a new stadium, but the plans fell on deaf ears."

Davis first recommended Schmittou to evaluate Huntsville Park, Optimist Park, and old airport land as potential facilities, but Schmittou ruled out Huntsville Park because of inadequate parking space and Optimist Park because of its antiquated state. Schmittou wanted a new stadium. So did Wallace, who saw a bigger picture of the new facility's use. He felt a new multiuse stadium would pay for itself through revenue from different sports. "Whether we get Minor League Baseball or not, the city of Huntsville needs a multipurpose stadium," Wallace said in 1982. "It's something we have been considering for a long time. I'm just hoping we can get someone else to listen to us."

A flurry of franchise movement in a complicated, three-league triangle made Wallace's dream of a new stadium come closer. Wallace, working for an engineering analysis firm, jumped back into the stadium talks in 1984 to serve behind the scenes as a liaison for Schmittou, Davis, and Southern League president Jimmy Bragan. Before Schmittou entered the narrative, rumblings of a franchise coming to Huntsville were already spreading fast. Reports circulated in early July that Steve Logan, a Marion County businessman, was bringing the Yankees' Double-A farm club to the city. The report made sense. New York needed to vacate Nashville and moving to Huntsville would keep them in the Southern League.

On July 6 the *Huntsville Times* reported that the city was on the verge of landing a pro baseball club. The rumor was that a Single-A team from the South Atlantic League would be moving to Huntsville and the announcement would be made by the end of the month. Wallace, actively searching for a pro franchise for the city, had been in talks with the Sally League and investors about bringing a Single-A club for some time. John Moss, the league's commissioner, was expanding to two more teams—from ten to twelve—in 1985 and eyed Huntsville as an expansion city. But Wallace never ruled out the possibility of a Double-A club, and Schmittou had created a vacancy in the Southern League days before when he purchased the Triplets. Schmittou's franchise remained an option for Rocket City. When Schmittou previously sparked discussions with city officials about bringing a team in 1982, they were gun-shy about paying for the new stadium that he required. They weren't ready to financially commit. "I talked with Mayor Davis there a few years ago, and there seemed to be interest in bringing a team to Huntsville, but there seemed to be no financial interest," Schmittou said in July 1984. "I left them my card and told them that if they ever had any interest in bringing a team to town, call me. I still have not heard from them." In fact, Schmittou was considering moving the franchise to Evansville to replace the Triplets.

Bringing baseball to Huntsville was just one of Davis's passions. The buzz about a new franchise came on the heels of the city's municipal election held on July 10, 1984. Mayor Davis, holding the seat since 1968, was seeking his last term as mayor and ran against longtime councilwoman Jane Mabry and councilman Bill Tallent. The fate of the election could significantly impact plans for a new stadium, especially if Davis lost. Another twist was that if a July 31 runoff was needed for Davis and either of his challengers, the delay could cost Huntsville the franchise. Mabry ran against Davis in 1980 and lost. In 1984 Mabry finished second in voting, again, and was only four votes shy of a July 31 runoff with Davis. Tommy Battle, Huntsville's mayor today, was the winner in the only City Council race, replacing Tallent in the five-member council.

Away from the campaign trails, Davis and Wallace were meeting with Logan to work on a deal to bring the Yankees' farm club. Logan, a resident of Hamilton Alabama, and Wallace were convinced the move would happen, and an official announcement was expected on July 12. The Single-A club rumored to be coming to Huntsville was awarded to Montgomery, leaving Double-A the likely option. The agreement with the Yankees would be contingent on Huntsville footing the bill for a new stadium. "I've been told that we do have the New York Yankees, if the city wants it," Wallace told the *Huntsville Times* in July 1984. "I have been told that the Yankees will make that official Thursday, or no later than next Monday." Davis scheduled a special meeting with the City Council about the million-dollar stadium project on the old airport property off South Memorial Parkway. The Southern League and New York reportedly even agreed to play home games at Huntsville Park until the new facility was built.

But when Logan failed to make the announcement and deliver the Yankees on July 12, some wondered if the move would ever happen. After all, it was Schmittou—not Logan—who owned the franchise and planned to move it to Evansville or Greensboro, North Carolina. Bragan was not thrilled about the Southern League losing the popular Nashville franchise and was not in favor of Evansville joining the league after failing to support a Triple-A club. Considering the movement of franchises, the timing and opportunity seemed perfect for Huntsville to host a Southern League club. If Huntsville landed a Double-A franchise, it became apparent that Logan would not be the one leading the charge. Schmittou was the one who could bring the franchise with the Southern League's approval.

Schmittou reunited with Huntsville officials on August 3, 1984, on the fifth floor of the municipal building, to meet about bringing his Nashville franchise. He presented the City Council of four men and one woman with another proposal to bring his franchise. He covered the terms of the lease agreement, including ticket sales, parking, and concessions that would be shared by the city and team. The city would be responsible for paying the upkeep and utilities of the stadium. Schmittou, also serving as marketing director for the Texas Rangers, assured the council that if they built him a ballpark, they would have a team by the following Monday. He wanted a deal in place with Huntsville by the time he met with the Southern League on August 13 and presented the move to Bragan.

Schmittou told the council the city would recoup the cost of the stadium in two years from increased sales tax revenue and that he would pay a $250,000 advance against rent for the first two years. He said the city would make most of the money from people visiting Huntsville for baseball. Not necessarily from ticket sales. He also forecasted the seventy-two home games in Huntsville would attract two hundred thousand fans per season, pumping $7 to $10 million in revenue annually into the economy. Some were suspect of Schmittou's projected attendance figures of over two hundred thousand, and as more details of the stadium were discussed, a snag suddenly emerged that soured the deal for the council: Schmittou insisted on beer sales at the new stadium during baseball games or he would not bring the franchise. "What happens if you don't have beer sales," council president Jimmy Wall asked Schmittou during the proposal. "If we don't have beer, we don't come," Schmittou responded. The consensus among Southern League owners was that a Minor League club couldn't survive without beer sales. Every stadium in the league sold beer in some fashion, although Greenville and Birmingham prohibited beer sales on Sundays. Both teams experienced a dip in attendance on Sundays.

Schmittou's latest requirement for a liquor-licensed facility was a major roadblock in negotiations. Once he mentioned beer sales, the council's tone changed. Cracks began to show in their support. Schmittou's ultimatum rubbed some of them the wrong way. Besides committing $2.5 to $3 million on a new stadium, agreeing to sell alcohol in the thick of the Bible Belt was discouraged. Beer sales at athletic events were prohibited under city ordinance at the time, and the assistant city attorney said it may take a special act of legislature to authorize beer sales.

Selling beer at the civic center was discussed in the past, but the city ordinance always prevented it. "Beer sales is one of the hardest things to accomplish," councilman Ernest Kaufmann said at the time. There were doubts the council even had the authority to change the ordinance. "It could be a hang-up," Davis said after the meeting. "It hasn't been the previous philosophy of this city to throw beer sales wide open." But in April 1981, Huntsville Speedway on Hobbs Road was granted a retail beer license since customers were bringing their own beer to the racetrack. In fact, the city collected beer tax revenue from the sales. The city not agreeing on beer sales would kill the deal, Schmittou warned.

The council told Schmittou they would decide and give him an answer when they convened the following Thursday evening, August 9. "Is it a bar operation, or is it an athletic activity?" Jane Mabry asked concerning Schmittou's demand to sell beer. Battle described the climate of buying, serving, and selling alcohol in Huntsville in the 1980s. "Back then, if you wanted to buy a bottle of wine in a grocery store, you had to go inside a room with curtains around it," recalled Battle. "You had to pick it up, place it inside a paper sack, and take it to the cashier's stand. You had to keep the alcohol bagged inside the grocery store because you didn't want to influence young people who might be in that store. There were many conservative churches in the area who were very much against alcohol."

On the same day Schmittou met with the city, Wallace, thirty-seven, announced his resignation as director of Parks and Recreation effective August 15. Having held that position since 1974, Wallace confirmed he was moving into the private sector but would still be available to consult city officials during baseball talks.

The council carefully weighed Schmittou's proposal as they grappled over beer sales. Some of them were skeptical of changing the city's attitude toward alcohol by allowing beer sales and how it could persuade other local businesses to want to sell it. Some were feeling reluctant to commit the old airport property to host sporting events, and others weren't completely convinced that Huntsville could support a baseball club as Schmittou insisted. They all agreed on the need for a multiuse stadium for local college and high school sports. "If he is so sure Huntsville will support it, then he should sign a lease to pay off the bond money the city will have to put up to build the stadium," councilman John Glenn said. "After that, we can talk about the schools and the universities using it." Another skeptic, Mabry, preferred that Schmittou spend money to improve Huntsville's existing fields. "There are doubters who say Minor League Baseball will not survive in this town, that Huntsville (along with outlying areas such as Decatur, Athens, and Scottsboro) will not support pro sports when its track record for supporting local teams is so suspect," wrote Mayes of the *Huntsville Times* in August 1984. But the political support from the University of Alabama and Alabama A&M and the Board of Education, who would benefit from using the new facility, could push the stadium into existence. The city agreed on the charm a new community sports facility would bring and recognized that eight of the ten Southern League cities had financed a new stadium for their team.

The talks appeared to have ended during the August 9 council meeting, however. The council expressed interest in a multiuse stadium, but after hearing concerns from local Protestant leaders and private citizens condemning alcohol sales, decided against serving alcohol in the proposed stadium in a unanimous 5–0 vote. One resident attending the session contended that selling beer at the stadium would lure more drunk drivers on city highways. The council advised that Schmittou could move the franchise to Huntsville, but the stadium would not sell beer for at least the first year. The notion was that while both parties continued talks on Schmittou's key demand, the city would compensate him for the financial impact of not selling beer the first season.

Schmittou rejected the counteroffer and claimed he was moving the franchise to Evansville. A defeated Davis marched out of the session and smoked a cigarette in the lobby. "I guess it's over," he said. "We've passed a golden opportunity to get a Double-A Southern League team. I don't know when another opportunity will come along. I don't think we can get a team as successful as the Nashville Sounds." Davis and Wallace revered Schmittou's track record and knew what kind of sparkling baseball world he would bring to the city. Nashville was a premier franchise, and Schmittou was one of baseball's top marketing minds.

Although Schmittou rejected the council's counteroffer, he didn't completely shut the door. He gave them an opportunity to change their mind. If they had second thoughts, he needed to hear from them by the following Monday—August 13 at 9:00 a.m.—when he was scheduled to meet with Southern League directors in Atlanta, Georgia. If Schmittou didn't hear from the city by then, he would inform the league he was moving the franchise to Evansville.

A highly publicized brawl between the San Diego Padres and Atlanta Braves on August 12 at Atlanta-Fulton County Stadium caused more concern for Schmittou's demand for beer sales. Seventeen players were ejected, and some fans fired beer at players from the stands. "That made it even more contentious," recalled Ernest Kaufmann. "It certainly didn't make it easier on some folks to vote."

But Davis, in eleventh-hour fashion, refused to give up. He revived talks over the weekend, and key councilmembers changed their tone and were more hopeful of working out a deal with Schmittou. Councilman Tallent, for example, recommended a designated nondrinker's section to accommodate beer sales. The consensus was that other points of the lease could be worked out. "Huntsville is starving to death for recreation and sports facilities and entertainment for youth," Tallent said in 1984. Only three council votes were needed to approve Schmittou's offer, and Davis felt he mustered enough support to seal the deal.

By Monday afternoon he scheduled a press conference: "We do have a ballclub," Davis told reporters. Councilmembers Glenn, Tallent, and Kaufmann approved controlled beer sales at the new stadium. The next step was for the council to sign the lease, and that would require approval by a majority. Final terms such as concessions, stadium maintenance, and rent still needed to be negotiated. Schmittou maintained he could start selling tickets for the 1985 season by late August if they approved the lease. Included in the eight-page lease were provisions for the sale and consumption of beer, restricted to sections agreed upon by the city for baseball games only, and reimbursement if the franchise did not come to Huntsville. "We set up a special alcohol-free section," recalled Battle. "Those who wanted to come and bring their church groups could be in there." The lease memorialized two weeks of negotiations. The city would grant Schmittou a ten-year lease with a ten-year option.

Davis called a special evening session with the council to ratify the lease on August 20, but Mabry voted against deciding on the lease, essentially killing the vote, so it was tabled until their regular Thursday session on August 23. Some of them wanted a copy of the lease in their hands to review. That Thursday evening, in the council chamber, with Schmittou on hand, the council approved the lease with a 4–1 vote in favor of building a multipurpose stadium on the north end of the old Huntsville airport property for Schmittou's franchise. "We weren't sure we were going to get a 4–1 vote; it looked more like a 3–2," Kaufmann said.

Wall, the council president, surprisingly made the motion to approve the agreement, and Mabry was the only one who opposed it. "Jane was a really good councilmember," Kaufmann said. "She voted with her convictions and didn't play games. If she felt strongly about something, that's just the way she felt. I had a lot of respect for her. She was reelected every time she ran except for the last time."

The city landed a baseball team, and after the vote, Schmittou asked Davis to throw out the ceremonial first pitch when the stadium opened. Davis willed the dream into existence with persistence and determination. The stadium would be named after him. "He pushed it hard and sold the council," Battle said. "It became a reality. When he spent almost 15 to 20 percent of his whole budget for the year on baseball, he took a big chance on someone named Larry Schmittou. Back in that day, we had a budget of about $31 to $32 million a year, and we ended up spending $3 to $6 million on the stadium by the time we finished with it. That was a huge percentage of everything we had. He did a great job."

Schmittou, meanwhile, was thrilled to bring his franchise to Huntsville, and said the club would have a country and western flavor like other clubs under his country music ownership group. Huntsville joined the Southern League's Western Division. "Beginning tomorrow we will start working on bringing a Southern League championship to Huntsville by next year," Schmittou said after the session.

If Schmittou brought a championship to Huntsville in 1985, the Yankees would not be associated with it, however. New York officials insisted that if Schmittou vacated Nashville, they would exercise a clause in their working agreement to pull their affiliation and not come with him. The partnership between the Yankees and Schmittou that started in Nashville in 1980 was ending. The Yankees were one of the selling points to bring the franchise to Huntsville. But the Yankees were eyeing moving their Double-A club to Albany, New York, and joining the Eastern League. New York already had a strong Triple-A affiliate in Columbus, Ohio. New York governor Mario Cuomo was pressuring Yankees owner George Steinbrenner to move the farm club to the state capital, if they ever vacated Nashville. Ben Bernard, who owned the Albany franchise, had built a new stadium in Albany—Heritage Park—in late 1983.

The move would bring them closer to the parent club in New York. Bernard loved the Yankees and was not renewing his affiliation with Oakland. So, he and the Yankees were close to a deal. Bernard wanted the farm club badly in Yankees country, and Schmittou saw the writing on the wall. "The Huntsville team may not be a Yankee ballclub," Schmittou warned. "We probably won't be a farm club for the Yankees. The Yankees will be given first rights to move their player development contract to Huntsville, but I look for them to move to Albany, New York." Schmittou promised to have a working agreement in place with another Major League club by mid-September.

Besides Schmittou's efforts on the Huntsville front, he was haggling with the league over the void of relocating the league's most lucrative franchise. But keeping the franchise in the league softened the blow. After paying Nashville a vacating fee and $250,000 to the league, he received approval to move the franchise to Huntsville. "It isn't like I was taking the franchise to a bad town," Schmittou said at the time.

"Huntsville would be among the top two or three places in the league in both attendance and facility. The next move is up to the Southern League. I'm going to be busy selling tickets."

As August gave way to September, the political clouds of cross-league franchise movement began to part, and the future looked clearer. The impetus of the musical chairs, Schmittou's purchase of the Triplets, had impacted four franchises and three leagues. When the Albany franchise officially announced a two-year working agreement with the Yankees on September 17, Bernard sold two hundred season tickets the same day. A day later, American Association president Joe Ryan announced that the Triple-A franchise in Evansville was moving to Nashville under Schmittou's ownership. Nashville had been a part of the Southern League since 1978. A club in Evansville no longer existed.

Schmittou began piecing together a front office staff for Huntsville. He named Don Mincher, a former Major Leaguer of thirteen seasons and Huntsville resident, as general manager on September 8. Like Myhand and Talley, Mincher was a baseball figurehead in Huntsville. Twenty-seven-year-old Kent Pylant, who worked for Schmittou in ticket sales in Nashville, was tapped as assistant general manager. Pylant, a Pulaski, Tennessee, native, was working as director of concessions for the Rangers at the time. After working in food and beverages, Pylant was anxious to be involved in baseball operations in Huntsville.

Huntsville officials, meanwhile, had chartered a plane to evaluate the site of the new 7,500-seat ballpark built in Greenville, but later found out it was being used only for baseball. The plan in Huntsville was for the stadium to be used for different sports. By September 13 the city had selected a local architect, Goodrum & Knowles, to design the stadium, and the city took out a temporary loan for short-term financing. While the base price of the stadium was $2.9 million, paved parking on thirty-four acres for 3,200 cars, and curbs, gutters, and drainages increased the total. The seats, bleachers, and benches also added to the base price. The stadium was constructed with prestressed concrete and movable seats to accommodate other sports. Goodrum & Knowles guaranteed the maximum cost of the stadium at $5.7 million and that the ballpark would be ready in time for baseball season, only six months away. The stadium's projected completion date was March 1,1985, with finishing touches completed by April 1. The city broke ground on September 21, 1984."The stadium was built in thirty-three and a half weeks," Rick Davis recalled.

With a new franchise coming and plans for a new ballpark in place, Schmittou soon found a Major League parent club. Walt Jocketty, an Oakland A's executive, visited Huntsville on September 14 to meet with franchise and city officials. He toured the site of the new stadium and met with the architectural firm. The new stadium was a selling point for Jocketty.

"I have been very impressed with what I've seen here today," Jocketty said in 1984. "The stadium looks like it will be beautiful, and I am impressed with the city driving around it. The stadium really has a chance to be one of the finer facilities in Minor League Baseball from what I've seen."

While New York was taking over Albany, Oakland needed a new Double-A affiliate. Oakland was one of four Major League clubs showing interest in sending a Double-A club with Schmittou to Huntsville. The Chicago Cubs, California Angels, and Cleveland Indians were the other clubs rumored. At least nine Double-A affiliate contracts expired after the 1984 season, and Oakland's contract with Bernard was one of them. "I visited Huntsville and saw what Larry was doing," remembered Jocketty. "He was bringing a franchise there and having a new stadium built. It looked like a great opportunity for us to go there and start a new relationship with the people."

Jocketty respected Schmittou's track record of building and branding a strong, first-class operation, but Schmittou was equally impressed with Oakland's farm system. Although the A's struggled at the big league level in 1984—finishing in fourth place under two managers— their farm system was flourishing. "Just because a team is doing well in their league doesn't mean that their Minor League organization is all that strong," Schmittou said in 1984. "Teams that are doing well at the big league level don't have as strong a need for strong Minor

League teams. Sometimes it's the teams that are a year or two away that have the best talent in their Minor Leagues. What we're looking for is a team that will provide us with the best talent to stock a club in Huntsville with."

Schmittou knew Oakland's farm system was on the rise and admitted they were high on his shopping list of clubs he wanted to bring. He always researched which clubs had the best players below the Double-A level, and Oakland's farm clubs were winning. But despite Oakland's premier farm system, the club Schmittou brought needed to meet three criteria: they must field a good team, must send solid citizens, and must bring the big league team to Huntsville for an exhibition game during the life of the contract. "Oakland qualifies in all three categories," Schmittou said in 1984. "Their Minor League system this year had the best win-loss record of any team with the exception of the New York Mets, and the A's were only a few percentage points behind." In fact, of Oakland's four lower-level clubs, only their Idaho Falls affiliate in the Pioneer (Rookie) League failed to make the play-offs, finishing at 29-41.

Jocketty and Schmittou had met during the winter meetings, but never partnered on a working agreement. Jocketty recognized that Schmittou was a smooth operator and was comfortable moving the farm club there. "We were looking at Midland, Texas, and the new franchise going into Huntsville," said Jocketty. "Midland was nice, and the owner was very nice. They had an older stadium that was in pretty good shape. But it was in the middle of nowhere in West Texas."

Schmittou and the A's agreed on a two-year working agreement in late September. Dating back to the 1960s, Oakland's Southern League Double-A affiliate once groomed stars for the parent club. About one hundred miles south of Huntsville, the Birmingham A's, Oakland's Double-A affiliate in Northern Alabama from 1967 to 1975, had streamed a crop of young superstars to Oakland. Rollie Fingers, Reggie Jackson, Vida Blue, and Joe Rudi all came through Birmingham during their ascent. They fueled the A's to three straight world championships from 1972 to 1974, including five consecutive division titles. Two decades later, Alabama would be another launching pad for Oakland's future stars.

Mincher, meanwhile, wanted community input to name Huntsville's new baseball team. He placed ads in local newspapers encouraging fans to mail in their name proposals, and after sifting through close to two thousand entries and narrowing it down to five finalists— the Stars, Satellites, Shuttles, Spacers, and Rockets—a committee of eleven local leaders led by Mincher, convincingly selected the Stars. The name symbolized Huntsville's identity with the space age and was sexy and marketable. "It was pretty much a unanimous choice," Pylant said after the announcement. "I think eight of the eleven voted on the Stars as their No. 1 choice. The people who didn't vote for the Stars first, voted them either second or third."

Schmittou's ownership group now boasted an impressive portfolio of four clubs in pro ball: a Triple-A franchise in Nashville, an existing Single-A one in Greensboro, North Carolina, an expansion one in Daytona Beach, Florida, and his newest in Huntsville. But whether Huntsville could support a pro franchise was still up in the air. Some doubted. Many wondered if joining forces with Oakland would make a difference. Some doubted the ballpark would be built in time for baseball in April. Only time would tell.

1. The Stars officially introduced Brad Fischer (*middle*) as manager and Gary Lance (*right*) as pitching coach during a press conference in Huntsville on November 12, 1984. General manager Don Mincher (*left*), Fischer, and Lance were thrilled about the new partnership in Huntsville. Alabama Department of Archives and History. Donated by Alabama Media Group. Photo by Dave Dieter, *Huntsville Times*.

2. (*opposite top*) Joe Davis Stadium was built as a multipurpose stadium to accommodate not only Minor League Baseball but also high school and college sports. The city broke ground on September 21, 1984, and Goodrum & Knowles, a local architecture firm, designed and built the stadium in only thirty-three weeks. Alabama Department of Archives and History. Donated by Alabama Media Group. Unknown photographer, *Huntsville Times*.

3. (*opposite bottom*) Construction staff worked long days to make Joe Davis Stadium baseball-ready for the home opener on April 19, 1985. Huntsville's brand-new stadium raised the bar for Minor League ballparks everywhere. Alabama Department of Archives and History. Donated by Alabama Media Group. Photo by Dave Dieter, *Huntsville Times*.

4. Fans formed long lines outside of the Huntsville Police Academy building to secure tickets before the season. The Stars sold over six thousand tickets that day. Alabama Department of Archives and History. Donated by Alabama Media Group. Photo by Dave Dieter, *Huntsville Times*.

5. Larry Schmittou was on hand when tickets for the home opener went on sale at their offices at the Huntsville Police Academy building on March 30, 1985. Alabama Department of Archives and History. Donated by Alabama Media Group. Photo by Dave Dieter, *Huntsville Times*.

6. (*opposite top*) The Stars' front office was busy on March 30, 1985, the first day of ticket sales. Many fans were excited about a visit from the San Diego Chicken in June. Alabama Department of Archives and History. Donated by Alabama Media Group. Photo by Dave Dieter, *Huntsville Times*.

7. (*opposite bottom*) The Stars first arrived in Huntsville on April 10, 1985. Jose Canseco walking on the airport runway with his A's equipment bag and radio, on the brink of having a legendary season at the plate. Alabama Department of Archives and History. Donated by Alabama Media Group. Unknown photographer, *Huntsville Times*.

8. (*opposite top*) During a tour of Joe Davis Stadium on April 10, 1985, Brian Graham (*left*) and Greg Cadaret (*right*) holding their new playing pants in the clubhouse, while Eric Plunk (*bottom*) sits and reads about Huntsville. Alabama Department of Archives and History. Donated by Alabama Media Group. Unknown photographer, *Huntsville Times*.

9. (*opposite bottom*) Oakland's Double-A farmhands arrived in Huntsville on April 10, 1985, and toured Joe Davis Stadium. Luis Polonia (*left*), Stan Javier, Eric Plunk, and Tim Belcher and his girlfriend, Teresa, evaluating the city's new state-of-the-art stadium that was soon dubbed the "Crown Jewel of the Southern League." Alabama Department of Archives and History. Donated by Alabama Media Group. Unknown photographer, *Huntsville Times*.

10. Rick Davis, the Stars' play-by-play voice, and Randy Davidson, the color commentator, smile from the broadcast booth at Rickwood Field on opening night. Alabama Department of Archives and History. Donated by Alabama Media Group. Photo by Dave Dieter, *Huntsville Times*.

11. During opening night pregame introductions at Birmingham's Rickwood Field on April 12, 1985, the Stars braced for their first season in franchise history. The club opened the season with eight road games while construction workers finished Joe Davis Stadium. In a Southern League slugfest, the Barons beat the Stars 15–12 and handed them their first loss of the season. Alabama Department of Archives and History. Donated by Alabama Media Group. Photo by Ed Jones, *Birmingham News*.

12. (*opposite top*) Brian Graham, second baseman for the Stars, was one of several Minor Leaguers who rose in Oakland's farm system in the early 1980s. Graham snatches a ball on the infield against the Birmingham Barons on April 12, 1985. Alabama Department of Archives and History. Donated by Alabama Media Group. Photo by Ed Jones, *Birmingham News*.

13. (*opposite bottom*) Rocky Coyle (*left*) and Chip Conklin (*right*) stretching and loosening up before opening night at Rickwood Field on April 12, 1985. They sparked Single-A Modesto to a California League championship in 1984 and made the talent-laden Double-A Huntsville club in 1985. Alabama Department of Archives and History. Donated by Alabama Media Group. Photo by Dave Dieter, *Huntsville Times*.

14. Joe Law firing a pitch on opening night against the Birmingham Barons. Boasting a formidable starting rotation of Law, Eric Plunk, Tim Belcher, Greg Cadaret, and Darrel Akerfelds, the Stars finished the first month of the season with a record of 14-5. Alabama Department of Archives and History. Donated by Alabama Media Group. Photo by Dave Dieter, *Huntsville Times*.

15. (*opposite top*) Joe Law was the starting pitcher on opening night against the Birmingham Barons. Law was a dazzling 11-2 with an earned run average of 2.58 for the Single-A Modesto A's in 1984. Law meeting with catcher Charlie O'Brien near the mound on opening night in 1985. Alabama Department of Archives and History. Donated by Alabama Media Group. Photo by Dave Dieter, *Huntsville Times*.

16. First baseman Rob Nelson swings away at Rickwood Field on opening night on April 12, 1985. Though Nelson belted two homers in the game, the Birmingham Barons outslugged the Stars 15–12. Alabama Department of Archives and History. Donated by Alabama Media Group. Photo by Dave Dieter, *Huntsville Times*.

17. (*opposite top*) Charlie O'Brien and Jose Canseco amusing each other during opening night ceremonies at Rickwood Field on April 12, 1985. Both ended up playing for the Oakland A's that season and had long Major League careers. Alabama Department of Archives and History. Donated by Alabama Media Group. Photo by Dave Dieter, *Huntsville Times*.

18. (*opposite bottom*) Leadoff batter Luis Polonia dashing into second base at Rickwood Field during opening night on April 12, 1985. Polonia, who set the table for the Stars' explosive lineup, finished the season with eighteen triples, one shy of the Southern League record at the time. Alabama Department of Archives and History. Donated by Alabama Media Group. Photo by Dave Dieter, *Huntsville Times*.

19. Enthusiastic fans lining up early for the home opener at Joe Davis Stadium on April 19, 1985. Over ten thousand fans crammed the new ballpark as the Stars filled a void for a community starving for summer entertainment. The club didn't disappoint and mauled the Birmingham Barons 10–0 that night. Alabama Department of Archives and History. Donated by Alabama Media Group. Photo by Dave Dieter, *Huntsville Times*.

20. Hundreds of fans waiting to enter Joe Davis Stadium for the first pitch of a new era of Huntsville baseball. The Stars drew over three hundred thousand fans in 1985, the franchise's first year of existence, and led the Southern League in attendance. Alabama Department of Archives and History. Donated by Alabama Media Group. Photo by Dave Dieter, *Huntsville Times*.

21. (*opposite top*) Mayor Joe W. Davis (*left*) was the man of the hour during the lively pregame ceremonies in Huntsville on April 19, 1985. Huntsville councilman Ernest Kaufmann presented Davis with a framed portrait of the new stadium dedicated to him for his determination to bring Rocket City a franchise. Davis, who passed away in 1992, threw out the ceremonial first pitch. Alabama Department of Archives and History. Donated by Alabama Media Group. Photo by Dave Dieter, *Huntsville Times*.

22. (*opposite bottom*) A young and focused Stars fan leaning on the dugout with his glove waiting for a ball during the home opener on April 19, 1985. Huntsville youth loved to come early and watch the Stars play after school. Alabama Department of Archives and History. Donated by Alabama Media Group. Photo by Dave Dieter, *Huntsville Times*.

23. (*opposite top*) Don Mincher—a former Major Leaguer and longtime Huntsville native—was named the first general manager of the Stars in September 1984. Mincher speaking to manager Brad Fischer in the dugout before a game at Joe Davis Stadium in 1985. Mincher was dubbed "Mr. Baseball" in Huntsville. Alabama Department of Archives and History. Donated by Alabama Media Group. Photo by Dave Dieter, *Huntsville Times*.

24. (*opposite bottom*) Organist Kathy Deaton, perched above the fans at Joe Davis Stadium, played fun tunes to celebrate professional baseball's return to Huntsville in 1985. Alabama Department of Archives and History. Donated by Alabama Media Group. Photo by Dave Dieter, *Huntsville Times*.

25. Rob Nelson drops a tag at first base during the first game ever at Joe Davis Stadium on April 19, 1985. Nelson, a left-handed power hitter, blasted thirty-two home runs for the Stars in 1985, third most in the Southern League that season. Alabama Department of Archives and History. Donated by Alabama Media Group. Photo by Dave Dieter, *Huntsville Times*.

26. (*opposite top*) Brad Fischer, manager of the Stars, compiled a record of 235-180 from 1982 to 1984 with the Madison Muskies—Oakland's Single-A affiliate in the Midwest League—before being promoted to managing Double-A Huntsville in 1985. Fischer (*above*) talking with his wife, Mary, before a game at Joe Davis Stadium in 1985. Alabama Department of Archives and History. Donated by Alabama Media Group. Photo by Dave Dieter, *Huntsville Times*.

27. (*opposite bottom*) Dozens of fans anxious to get their hands on an official souvenir program before the home opener in 1985. Only eight months had passed since Huntsville was awarded the Southern League franchise. Alabama Department of Archives and History. Donated by Alabama Media Group. Photo by Dave Dieter, *Huntsville Times*.

28. Former Major Leaguer Bob Watson was one of Oakland's four roving Minor League instructors in 1985. The A's hired him after he retired in 1984. Boasting a career batting average of .295, Watson coached several Huntsville players on hitting. Alabama Department of Archives and History. Donated by Alabama Media Group. Photo by Dave Dieter, *Huntsville Times*.

29. Centerfielder Stan Javier played briefly with the New York Yankees in 1984 and was the only player on the Stars with Major League experience. Javier sitting on the top step of the dugout before the home opener. He lived on the bases in 1985 and boasted an on-base percentage of .419. Alabama Department of Archives and History. Donated by Alabama Media Group. Photo by Dave Dieter, *Huntsville Times*.

30. Gary Lance served as pitching coach for the Single-A Madison Muskies in 1984, and manager Brad Fischer brought him to Huntsville in 1985 to work with Oakland's Double-A hurlers. Alabama Department of Archives and History. Donated by Alabama Media Group. Photo by Dave Dieter, *Huntsville Times*.

31. Shortstop John Marquardt turning a double play against the Birmingham Barons at Joe Davis Stadium. The Stars, in their inaugural season, were Western Division champions of the first half by virtue of a 39-32 record. Alabama Department of Archives and History. Donated by Alabama Media Group. Photo by Dave Dieter, *Huntsville Times*.

32. The franchise left Huntsville after the 2014 season and relocated to Biloxi, Mississippi, and was named the Biloxi Shuckers. The Rocket City Trash Pandas, the Double-A club of the Los Angeles Angels, arrived in Madison, Alabama, in 2020. Players lined up during the national anthem at Toyota Field in 2021. Courtesy of Lucas Dolengowski / Rocket City Trash Pandas.

5

New Kids on the Block

"Our newspaper was fired up about covering the A's that spring. We wanted to cover Tim Belcher and Rob Nelson. We heard things about Darrel Akerfelds because of his Lou Holtz football connection at the University of Arkansas. Stan Javier was interesting because his dad, Julian, was a former Major Leaguer, and Stan had already played for the Yankees in 1984."
—**BOB MAYES**, former beat writer, *Huntsville Times*, February 2007

Brad Fischer made the Madison Muskies the pride of Oakland's farm system—the model hub of the organization. He was one of Minor League Baseball's winningest managers. The twenty-eight-year-old manager of the A's Single-A club in Wisconsin led them to three consecutive winning seasons since taking over the new franchise in 1982. He twice piloted the Muskies to the Midwest League playoffs after managing Oakland's short-season Single-A club in Medford, Oregon, from 1980 to 1981. The Blissfield, Michigan, native posted an overall record of 235-180 for the Muskies from 1982 to 1984, boasting a .556 winning percentage. He began managing in Oakland's organization at age twenty-three. In five seasons, Fischer had a 299-256 record.

He was a rising managerial star in the organization. As Oakland's top prospects moved up the chain, so did Fischer. In November 1984, Oakland promoted him to Double-A. He was managing the A's new farm club in Huntsville that came from Albany. Like he experienced in Madison, Fischer was managing the franchise's first year of existence in Huntsville. "He was a young, successful Minor League manager and moving up along with the prospects," said Walt Jocketty. "He won everywhere he went. He related well with young players and was a good teacher." In corresponding moves, Keith Lieppman, who managed in Albany in 1984, was promoted to manage Triple-A Tacoma. Jim Nettles replaced Fischer in Madison.

Not everyone was thrilled about Oakland's managerial shuffling that winter. George Mitterwald, the thirty-nine-year-old manager of Oakland's Single-A club in Modesto who led them to a California League championship in 1984, figured he would be the one promoted to Double-A. After all, Modesto was the A's only farm club to win a championship in 1984. Mitterwald's record was 158-120 in two seasons at Modesto. But he learned from Oakland he would be managing in Modesto for a third consecutive season. "I really didn't think I'd be back," Mitterwald said at the time. "Not that I don't like Modesto. I really enjoy Modesto . . . but I was hoping to move up in the organization, I'm kind of disappointed I didn't." He was starting to wonder where he stood in Oakland's plans. In 1982, after the A's fired Billy Martin, they involuntarily moved Mitterwald from big league bullpen coach to manage Modesto.

Mitterwald was another one of Martin's friends, and his philosophy on winning clashed with Oakland's new focus on player development. And Karl Kuehl, the A's new director of player development, had the juice to enforce it. "Karl told me he wasn't totally happy with the job that I did, that I was placing too much emphasis on winning and not enough on developing players," Mitterwald told the *Modesto Bee* in 1984. As Kuehl shook up the farm system, the highly favored Fischer and Lieppman were positioned to be Oakland's future.

Fischer grew up in the A's organization and his relationship with Oakland can be traced to the final days of Charlie Finley's ownership. Being an undrafted catcher from Western Michigan University in 1978 didn't create much opportunity for him to play pro ball. But he attended an A's tryout and made their rookie club in Bend, Oregon. Playing in the Northwest League, the passed balls piled up, however, and Fischer, twenty-two, was released after only one season. Fischer was out of baseball in 1979 and worked for an engineering company in

Jackson, Michigan. He doubted he would ever return to baseball until Oakland called. Norm Koselke, Oakland's farm director at the time and a cousin to Finley's wife, and Ed Nottle, his former manager in Bend, offered him an option to stay in the game. "Ed had asked me if I was interested in coaching or managing," recalled Fischer. Recognizing his playing days were over and seeing the writing on the wall, Fischer decided to accept the challenge. "Lo and behold, Koselke called me in the middle of the winter and hired me as manager of the short-season club in Medford," said Fischer. "He was an old Charlie Finley guy." Fischer replaced Rich Morales.

The twenty-three-year-old manager needed to quickly switch from player-and-teammate mode to manager and disciplinarian. Adjusting to his new role as skipper—especially being so young—took time.

"I had to suddenly manage a handful of my former teammates from a year before," he said. "Managing so young was interesting. As a former player, I knew some things players were involved in that they probably didn't want me to know as manager. I had to make tough decisions, which made it uncomfortable. But for the most part, I didn't have any problems. I liked the players and spent a lot of time working with them."

Managing in Medford in 1980 was a learning curve for the rookie manager filled with first-time experiences. Before the June post-draft summer season, Fischer walked into a decaying and neglected A's farm operation. In fact, he needed to hold his own tryout just to field a team, something he never did before. He signed fourteen players from the tryout. Medford finished fourth in the short-season Northwest League's South Division by virtue of a 22-48 record under Fischer. The forty-eight losses were the most ever for the franchise. "Being a young manager was not easy, especially my first year," admitted Fischer. "You could see it reflected in our win-loss record." Before Medford's season started on June 15, Fischer traveled to California and assisted Lieppman's Single-A club in Modesto as a coach. "Brad was a young guy just starting off, so he had some hurdles to overcome," said Lieppman. "Some of his players were almost his age. He had good character and was disciplined. He set good boundaries for his team and had fun.

Mixing discipline and fun is a part of the whole equation to building relationships. Brad put together all of those things to accomplish what he did as a manager."

The following season, in 1981, Fischer turned the club around. He led Medford to a Northwest League championship. At the peak of "Billy Ball" in Oakland, Fischer piloted Medford to a 42-28 record before Oakland promoted him to manage the Muskies in 1982. Managing his first full 140-game season, Fischer fell in love with Madison right away and brought winning baseball for three straight years. He owned a condo in Madison with wife, Mary, and son, Danny, three. Fischer was adored in Madison, and he embraced the community. "We lived right across the street from the ballpark and ended up making Madison our home," said Fischer. "The club was new in town, and there was enthusiasm every night. We had good teams and all the pieces fell into place."

Fischer's stock in Oakland's organization was rising fast and his dream of managing in the big leagues was coming closer. He was dependable and consistent. During organizational shakeups and firings when Kuehl was cleaning house, Fischer held Madison down with excellence. The capital Fischer had built in the organization was enough to warrant his second promotion as a manager. Sandy Alderson, Jocketty, and Kuehl tapped him to manage the new Huntsville club. But leaving Madison for a promotion was bittersweet. He reflected on managing in Madison before he left. "There isn't a better city to manage a Class A team in than Madison," Fischer said at the time. "That's what has made it easier to stay at this level for so long." Fischer had never managed a losing team except for his first year in Medford in 1980. "Brad grew up in the organization and was a good baseball guy," said Grady Fuson, a coach and scout for Oakland in the 1980s. "He was a part of the top-tier of instructors we had during that era."

Fischer had never seen a Double-A game in his life, but he was anxious to travel to Huntsville for a November 12 press conference introducing the new club and his promotion as manager. "We fell in love with Huntsville," remembered Fischer. "They were very accommodating and loving people. I was thrust into an ideal situation." Gary Lance, Fischer's pitching coach in Madison, came with him to Huntsville to serve in the same role. "To me, it's like starting pro baseball all over again," Fischer said in 1985. "I'm in a new city, we're going to have a great new stadium, it's a step up for me. I know it's going to be a big challenge."

Fischer was emblematic of the rising stars Oakland was on the verge of sending to Huntsville. A month later, more hot prospects were positioned to be in Rocket City. During the winter meetings in Houston, Texas, on December 5, 1984, Oakland landed a smorgasbord of premier prospects from the Yankees for superstar Rickey Henderson, twenty-five, and Bert Bradley, a pitcher who was 10-2 for Triple-A Tacoma in 1984. To acquire Henderson, New York sent Oakland five players: fire-balling reliever Jay Howell, twenty-eight; three top pitching prospects, Jose Rijo, nineteen; Eric Plunk, twenty-one; Tim Birtsas, twenty-four; and switch-hitting outfielder Stan Javier, twenty. Javier and Rijo had a cup of coffee with New York in 1984, while the older, well-traveled Howell, who boasted a 9-4 record for the Yankees in 1984, had pitched for the Cincinnati Reds, Chicago Cubs, and New York since 1980. The towering Plunk, six feet six, and Birtsas, six feet seven, the only ones without any Major League experience, pitched for New York's Single-A affiliate in Fort Lauderdale in 1984. Birtsas, a lefty, was 5-1 with a 3.59 earned run average, while Plunk, a righty, posted a 12-12 record and earned run average of 2.86, leading the Florida State League in strikeouts. Birtsas, who starred for Michigan State University, was New York's first pick of the 1982 draft. The Dominican Republic-born Rijo, who was fifteen years of age when he signed a professional contract with the Yankees in 1981, featured an explosive fastball, but his control was erratic. In 1983 eighteen-year-old Rijo was 15-5 with a 1.68 earned run average in the Florida State League and was crowned New York's Minor League pitcher of the year.

The bold trade punctuated Oakland's commitment to develop for the future, but the A's were also losing money every year and needed to cut ties with large salaries associated with superstars like Henderson. They had lost $5.5 million in 1984 and expected to lose another $25 million over the next three years. They had not had a winning season since 1981. Trading Henderson was inevitable. Henderson, a hometown hero represented by agent Richie Bry, was slated to be a free agent after the 1985 season, and Oakland contended they couldn't afford him any longer. So rather than losing him for nothing after the 1985 season, they got a haul of prospects for him in return. It was one of the first blockbuster superstar-for-prospects trades of its kind. "We felt it was unlikely, in the San Francisco-Oakland market, we could afford Rickey," Roy Eisenhardt, president of the A's, said after the trade. "It is possible players of Rickey's ability are affordable under the present configuration only by clubs in bigger markets and by clubs owning television superstations."

George Steinbrenner was thrilled to have acquired Henderson, his new leadoff batter and centerfielder. "Rickey Henderson is a player of tremendous charisma and excitement," he announced after the trade. "He will really turn on our great New York Yankee fans, and we are really eager to put him in the lineup with our other players so he can do just that."

Sandy Alderson, the A's former general manager, recalled pulling the trigger on the seven-player trade. "We had been talking to the Dodgers about Rickey as an alternative to the Yankees," Alderson said. "We weren't getting very far, so Clyde King and Woody Woodward of the Yankees jumped in. The deal was complicated because we had to get Rickey to agree to the trade. Because I wasn't all that confident in our scouting information, I reviewed a copy of *Baseball America*. It listed the Yankees' top ten prospects." Alderson analyzed the list like a kid in a candy store and got almost everything he wanted. "I told them I wanted their top five prospects for Rickey," said Alderson. "I just went down the list. My guess is that we got five of their top seven prospects." The Yankees refused to give up catching prospect Scott Bradley, regarded as their catcher of the future, in the trade. Henderson signed a five-year, $8.75 million pact with New York.

Two of Oakland's new prospects from New York, Plunk and Javier, would later be dispatched to Huntsville to open the 1985 season. Javier was the son of Julian Javier, former St. Louis Cardinal second baseman. Javier had a dazzling season in 1983 playing for the Single-A Greensboro

Hornets as a nineteen-year-old. He hit .311 with twelve homers and swiped thirty-three bases in 129 games. The Yankees even called him up briefly in 1984 after playing for Triple-A Columbus. Javier expected his future to be with the Yankees. "The Yankees seemed to have big plans for us, but I heard they wanted a leadoff hitter," said Javier. "So, they sent a bunch of prospects to Oakland for Rickey, and I was one of them." The Yankees boasted the highest payroll in baseball—$11.7 million—in 1984, and Javier immediately noticed a different mentality in Oakland, ranked ninth in that category. "Everything was winning, winning, winning with the Yankees," said Javier. "They kept players a long time because they just wanted to win. Because you needed to perform there right away, there was a lot more pressure on you. Oakland, on the other hand, wanted to build the team around prospects. Everything had to be the biggest and the best with the Yankees. Oakland was more careful about spending."

Javier joined the A's at the onset of their partnership with Larry Schmittou, who just convinced them to plant their Double-A farm club in Huntsville. Schmittou knew Oakland's system was loaded with talent. He always studied which clubs had the best prospects coming up and marveled at Oakland's crop at Single-A. "I had selected Oakland because they had outstanding players coming up from Single-A," he recalled. "Most of those guys came from Modesto a year before and won a championship. I knew the next step for them was Double-A."

Modesto was coming off a championship season in 1984, and the core of the club was moving up in 1985. The Stars were composed mostly of players with winning experience from farm stops in Medford, Albany, Madison, and Modesto. "We had won in Medford a few years earlier with some of those same guys," remembered Jocketty. "Back then, my philosophy was winning and developing go hand in hand. To develop winning players, you need to have winning teams. Winning helped their transition."

Lieppman credited Oakland's rigorous offseason programming in Arizona for shaping their development and ascent. "By the time Brad took over that team, those players had been through a little bit of that process through instructional leagues," said Lieppman. "It aided them in their ability to go quickly through a system. It was a sign our system was coming to life. We really didn't have a lot of success with our drafts in the early 1980s. We started getting good results from trades. It was outstanding seeing those guys come through our system. The young players benefited greatly from the new system Sandy and Karl brought. It was a great time for innovation in our organization."

But Oakland's new approach still needed to prove successful on the field. Fischer and Lance reported to spring training in Scottsdale on March 8, while pitchers reported on March 12, and position players, March 16. Lance had already spent some time in Huntsville after coaching winter ball in Puerto Rico. Spring training took on a new look. Oakland's Minor League managers and instructors attended two days of classroom instruction on sports psychology before the players arrived to take physicals. Newly hired Harvey Dorfman was anointed to lead the charge on emphasizing mental awareness to the organization at the Minor League camp. "Dorfman kept us grounded," said Jose Canseco. "If we had any overwhelming issues as younger players, he was there to help us out. He was a nice guy."

Before spring training, Fischer envisioned twenty-two-year-old Darrel Akerfelds, his pitching ace in Madison the previous season, highlighting Huntsville's staff. The right-hander was 11-6 for Fischer in 1984. Akerfelds was Seattle's first-round selection in 1983 before being traded to Oakland. "He was a manager's delight," recalled Fischer. "Any manager in the world would enjoy managing him. He was a tough competitor." First baseman Rob Nelson, infielder John Marquardt, and third baseman Terry Steinbach also came from Madison to join Fischer in Huntsville.

Fischer indicated the roster would be set by late March. The forecast for the organization was power and pitching. That spring, Kuehl made it clear that Oakland's four new roving Minor League instructors would be the foundation of the farm system under his direction. Ron Plaza, a former coach with the Reds, Fred "Chicken" Stanley, a former infielder for the Yankees and A's, and Bob Watson, a slugger who retired after the 1984 season after a nineteen-year career in the Majors, were introduced as the instructors along with Dorfman. "Karl demanded excellence," said Brian Dorsett, a catcher drafted by Oakland in 1983. "He was a manager before in Montreal and had been around the block. He had a presence about him and demanded respect. He wasn't going to have any slackers around him and made sure everyone knew it."

Brian Guinn, a shortstop in Oakland's organization for four years, remembered working under Plaza. "If you wanted to put in extra work, Ron was going to be there for you," said Guinn. "I remember trying to learn how to push bunt and asked him to help me out. He told me that if I got to the park at 7:00 a.m., he'd help me. So, I got to the park at 6:30 a.m. thinking I would beat him there, but he was already standing there waiting for me."

Watson, who clubbed 184 homers during his career, was a former marine drill instructor and now Oakland's Minor League hitting instructor. "Bob became one of my mentors when he got there," said Guinn. "He used to always sit me down and talk about different approaches to the game. He even tried to get me in big league camp one year." Kuehl hired Watson in November 1984 to replace Willie Horton, a former Major Leaguer. Watson and Kuehl were no strangers. In 1964 Kuehl, then a Houston scout, signed Watson to his first professional contract with the Astros. Watson also received an offer to stay in the Braves organization, but he accepted Kuehl's offer. Watson, an Atlanta, Georgia, resident, planned on spending a lot of time roaming the Southern League to evaluate prospects in Huntsville. "I had an offer from the Braves, but with the A's, I'm going to have a little more flexibility," Watson said in 1985. "I'll get to cross a few lines. I'll be doing some scouting and special assignments for the big club in addition to working with the Minor League teams."

Stanley was the director of instruction. Dorfman was also available for players dealing with personal matters. Working under Kuehl, the instructors were assigned to rotate through A's affiliates during the season to evaluate the progress of prospects. Don Mincher, the newly minted general manager of the Stars, was in Scottsdale to check out potential players bound for Huntsville. The Stars were opening the season on the road against the Birmingham Barons on April 12 before the highly anticipated home opener in the new stadium on April 19. There, Mincher sold the players on Huntsville and the new stadium. "Everyone wanted to go to Huntsville," remembered Guinn. "The city had a new facility, and everything was brand new, but we knew everyone couldn't go."

It was on Field No. 2 at Scottsdale Community College where A's Minor Leaguers—one hundred of them—assembled for spring training. Oakland's Major League camp, which included about forty players, was held at Phoenix Municipal Stadium, a few miles away from Scottsdale. "Our newspaper was very fired up about covering the A's that spring," the late Bob Mayes, former Stars beat reporter for the *Huntsville Times*, said in 2007. "We wanted to cover Tim Belcher and Rob Nelson. We heard things about Akerfelds because of his Lou Holtz football connection at the University of Arkansas."

Oakland's new instructors—Plaza, Watson, Stanley, and Dorfman—went right to work schooling A's Minor Leaguers that spring. They stressed hard work and opened camp with conditioning and drills. The pitchers tossed easy and batting practice began immediately. Lance made sure his pitchers did sit-ups every day. Kuehl, meanwhile, watched closely to ensure the focus of instruction was on player development and character, not just winning on the diamond. They even rolled out interpersonal skills workshops for players. Kuehl, Fischer, Lance, and the instructors worked out of a small trailer on the grounds of the community college.

Not every A's Minor Leaguer was in Scottsdale that spring. Jose Canseco, twenty, was in big league camp in Phoenix for the first time. Canseco, a strapping, tall, power-hitting outfield prospect, had posted promising offensive numbers for Modesto in 1984. But tragedy struck during the summer. Canseco had lost his mother, Barbara, thirty-six, from a brain tumor in July, and after missing three weeks of playing time because of the tragedy, he helped muscle Modesto to a championship when he returned. He led Modesto with fifteen home runs and seventy-three RBIs. Canseco remembered how the tragedy of losing his mother unfolded:

"I was struggling in Modesto and kind of lost my way in the game," said Canseco. "I didn't want to play anymore. I wasn't really putting up good stats and was kind of homesick. Everything was going wrong for me. My mom had suffered from migraine headaches, but I never really knew how bad. My sister suddenly called me and told me I'd better fly home right now because my mom was very sick. But she didn't tell me why. So, I grabbed a flight the next morning.

I flew in and they took me to Mount Sinai Hospital to see my mom. I went into this room and my mom was connected to this machine that was artificially keeping her body alive. She was basically already dead. She was brain dead. When I saw her, I lost my mind and started crying. My mom had never seen me play pro ball and never experienced that kind of game. Right then and there, I promised her I would be the best player in the world for her."

Because of that promise, Canseco said he began using performance enhancing drugs during the offseason to get bigger, stronger, and faster. He packed on slabs of muscle to his skinny frame during the winter and strutted into spring training looking like the Incredible Hulk. "Canseco put on fifty pounds and looked like a giant," recalled Dorsett. "He didn't need to, but he did. Baseball hadn't seen anything like it." Canseco made noise early in the spring. He clobbered a massive two-run homer to dead center off A's pitcher Chris Codiroli in Phoenix to fuel the "B" team during the first intra-squad game. The blast set the tone for his legendary season. His freakish power raised eyebrows in camp. "He was a good player before he was on steroids," said Charlie O'Brien, "but when he got on steroids, it took him to another level. I played with him a few games in Modesto in 1984 and he really didn't stand out. He only weighed about 195 pounds. He came to spring training weighing 245 pounds and looked like a totally different person. Balls were exploding off his bat like crazy."

As impressive as Canseco's power was, Eric Plunk's explosive fastball was equally noteworthy. But as lively as his right arm was, he battled wildness, which frightened batters at times. Facing Plunk was scary. He threw gas and was wild. He wore Coke-bottle glasses on the mound, and his control problems scared hitters because he threw so hard. When Plunk fired the ball, no one knew where it was going. Not even Plunk sometimes. He coughed up 123 walks and 17 wild pitches in 176 innings in 1984. "He wore these very thick glasses, and was very scary," remembered Rick Stromer, a third baseman for the Stars in 1985. "He didn't have any idea where he was throwing the ball. It was insane." But Plunk's heat and intimidating presence on the mound made him a promising prospect. He needed to develop consistency.

Like Canseco, Plunk, Javier, and O'Brien, a catcher, were also invited to big league camp. On March 24 the A's optioned them to Minor League camp. While many A's prospects were excited to play in Double-A, not all of them were. Some of them had their sights on cracking Triple-A, and ultimately, the big leagues. O'Brien, for example, had already played in sixty-nine games for Triple-A Tacoma in 1984 and was bummed he was starting the season in Huntsville. He wanted to at least start the season in Tacoma. But Oakland wanted him and Bill Bathe, Tacoma's catcher, to play every day. One bright spot for O'Brien that spring was Don Sutton, Oakland's veteran starting pitcher, tossed a lot of Double-A games and O'Brien was his catcher of choice. Sutton raved about O'Brien to A's manager Jackie Moore. But when the season started, Bathe was the one in Tacoma and O'Brien was in Huntsville. "I was pissed off," said O'Brien. "I had already played in Triple-A Tacoma the year before. They told me Bill was older, so they were going to give him his last chance. I was disappointed because I felt like they lied to me. I was caught up in a regime change."

Javier, too, was troubled over being sent to Huntsville. "I was very pissed off because I had already played in Double-A a year before," Javier said. "I had a great spring training and hit a couple of home runs. I was killing Triple-A pitching in Scottsdale, and they still sent me down to Double-A. I didn't understand why at first, but later found out they wanted to keep the prospects together." Stromer recalled

Javier's frustration. "Stan was a little standoffish," he said. "Being traded to the A's was a slap in the face. It was more difficult for him."

By the time the Stars broke spring training on April 9, most of Oakland's top farmhands were headed to Huntsville. "Oakland wanted to have a good team going into a good city," said O'Brien. "There's no doubt that some of our guys could have been playing in Triple-A. One of their intentions was to put a great team there, and they did." Oakland sent a batch of fireballing prospects to Huntsville: Plunk, six feet six; Belcher, six feet three; Greg Cadaret, six feet three; Akerfelds, six feet two; and Joe Law, six feet two, made up the starting rotation. The composition of the staff generated enthusiasm. On fireballers Plunk, Belcher, and Akerfelds specifically, A's scout Ron Schueler marveled: "They're going to shoot three guys at you that shoot ninety-two miles per hour." The highly touted Belcher was twice the first pick of the draft in 1983–84 and had a strong first season in the Minors in 1984. Fischer broke camp with a ten-man pitching staff. John Marquardt was Huntsville's shortstop. His father, John Sr., was a team physician for the Chicago Cubs.

The club wasn't composed of all tall, headlining prospects, however. Tough twenty-five-year-old outfielder Rocky Coyle, standing at only five feet eight and weighing 180 pounds, made the Stars as a utility outfielder. Coyle, the oldest player on the club, was slated to back up the starting outfield of Luis Polonia, Javier, and Canseco. Coyle was happy to be playing Double-A. "All the talent was in Double-A," Coyle said. While he was embarking on his fourth season in pro ball, the odds were against him to make the Majors. He wasn't considered a prospect or on Oakland's radar. After all, besides being short in stature in the baseball world, he was older than a lot of players on the parent club in Oakland. Plus, playing in a system filled with prospects stiffened the competition. He was always told he was a good "little" ball player. "Coyle was a great guy, but he didn't have the prospect measurements that Oakland was looking for," said John Pruett, who covered him in 1985. "He wasn't 6'2" or 6'3." He was 5'8" on a good day, but he was scrappy and played hard." Speedy outfielder Polonia was five feet eight and part of Oakland's plans, but he was only twenty and considered to have more upside.

Coyle was not considered an underdog growing up. He dominated. The hard-nosed Coyle was a sparkplug everywhere he played since starring on neighborhood sandlot leagues in Phoenix, Arizona, as a ten-year-old boy. He competed with sixteen-year-olds, and his baseball IQ grew fast. "Being the youngest kid there, the older guys took me under their wing," said Coyle. "By the time I started playing little league, I was already an excellent player. I was fast and could always hit."

Born to Terence and Susan, on February 23, 1960, Rocky Joseph Coyle was the second of five children: Kevin, Maureen, Danny, and Katie, in that birth order. Coyle looked up to the eldest, Kevin, a stand-out pitcher, shortstop, and basketball player. "I kind of idolized my brother. That's probably why I'm here where I am. I looked up to him. He was one of the best shortstops I had ever seen," Coyle said in 1982.

Young Rocky was always the toughest out in little league and striking him out was a milestone and headache for every pitcher. It never happened. Even his teammates respected the oddity. "The first time I struck out in little league, everyone in the stands was cheering and I didn't understand why," Coyle said. "My own teammates were cheering because it was so difficult to get me out. I cried on the field. I didn't understand why parents in the stands were glad I got out." Coyle credited his father, Terence, for guiding him through the trauma of failing for the first time. "I felt embarrassed, like I failed my dad, and went straight to my bedroom and started crying," he remembered. Terence himself was no stranger to the pressures of competing in sports. Before coaching, he was a boxer and starting point guard for the University of Arizona's basketball squad from 1955 to 1957. He called Rocky "Rock." "He looked me in the eyes and told me, 'Let me tell you this early in life, Rock. I don't care if you get four hits in a game, if you're an All-American, or if you even play pro ball. I love you because you're my son. I'm proud of you, no matter what.'" Terence's charge comforted and inspired Coyle. He felt security and was committed to pouring his life onto the field no matter what. "My dad was a great man and coach," Coyle said. "He was the real foundation that made me a great player."

The pep talk apparently worked. On the field, Coyle hustled and dominated. He played eager, anxious, and antsy. He left everything on the field and played with all his heart. "He was super aggressive and played the game hard," Fischer remembered. "He always gave 100 percent." Coyle hit over .400 each of his three years at Coronado High School in Scottsdale, Arizona, and hit .393 and .398 in two years at Mesa Community College. In high school, he starred in baseball, football, and basketball. He was a running back in football and a guard in basketball. In baseball, he was crowned the *Arizona Republic*'s Class AAA Player of the Year in 1978. He played hard and loved his teammates. He never struck out during his senior year in high school. In his final year at Mesa, he broke the school RBI record and was an All-American outfielder. But pro scouts never paid much attention to him, and he went undrafted each of those years. Rocky's formula for success never showed up in scouting reports. Some compared him to Pete Rose, nicknamed "Charlie Hustle," because he played the game with childish joy and loved dirtying up a uniform. He banged into outfield fences and flew headfirst into bases. "My journey has always been a battle," remembered Coyle.

Coyle did, however, receive a full baseball scholarship from UA for his final two college years and hit over .300 in each of those seasons. He was also able to pursue his education as opposed to jumping right into pro ball. He later earned a bachelor's degree in psychology and physical education from Liberty University in 1992.

The speedy Coyle, serving as co-captain, put the ball in play. In fact, during his final season playing for the Wildcats, Coyle had a stretch of over 140 at bats without a strikeout, along with a .361 batting average, the highest in the Southern Division of the Pac-10. He was a hitting machine and was given the impression he would be drafted. But when the 1982 June Amateur Draft came around, he was again ignored by every Major League club. Jerry Kindall, Coyle's coach at UA, had even alerted five farm directors about Coyle before the draft, but he wasn't among the more than 830 players selected. Kindall was also pushing for outfielder Jim Bagnall, another Wildcats player not drafted. "I'm puzzled by it," Kindall said in 1982. "You couldn't find two more prized young men in terms of ability, personality, and character. But I'll continue to try and find at least a tryout for them." Another reason Coyle and Bagnall might have been overlooked was because the Wildcats failed to make the College World Series in 1982. Only two Wildcats players were drafted in the regular phase that year—pitchers Ed Vosberg and Ron Sismondo.

Coyle said he would play pro ball for nothing. He pursued a career in baseball and signed as a free agent in July 1982 with the Utica Blue Sox of the New York Penn League, an independent club partially owned by comedian and actor Bill Murray. Coyle fueled the club to a New York Penn League championship in 1983. He batted .381, clubbed sixteen home runs, and swiped eighteen bases. He also had an on base percentage of .425. "I got an opportunity to play there right out of college," said Coyle. "I didn't get signed by a Major League club in 1982 and came back the following season and did well. We won the championship as an independent club." A few pro scouts were finally interested in Coyle, twenty-three, and Dick Wiencek, the A's scouting director, was one of them. He signed Coyle and sent him to play for Modesto in 1984. "You had to fight your way up to let people know you could play," Coyle said. And he did just that.

Playing in the Golden State under George Mitterwald in 1984, Coyle didn't skip a beat. He was an All-Star and willed Modesto to a championship. In 124 games Coyle hit .296 and led the club with 130 hits. He was 10 for 29 in the playoffs. The club also included Canseco and Mark McGwire, Oakland's first-round selection— tenth overall—who reported to Modesto in August after playing in the Los Angeles Olympics. "We weren't supposed to win," Coyle said. "Oakland really loaded up Madison. They had a great team." Madison finished in second place. "Given the opportunity, I excelled everywhere I went," he said. Coyle's hustle and leadership on and off the field inspired the club. He said Mitterwald inspired him. "He was a great manager," said Coyle. "He came from the Billy Martin era in Oakland and loved his players. Our group of guys really loved each other."

While the twenty-two-man roster was in place, back in Huntsville the city was bustling with anticipation. Over 1,500 season tickets had already been sold. But the elephant in the room was whether the city's $5.7 million stadium would be ready in time for the April 19 home opener. After one thousand stadium bleacher seats were destroyed by fire on March 9, replacements took two weeks to arrive. The fierce winter weather had resulted in days of delay. Manpower of over two hundred workers from twenty-eight subcontractors worked tirelessly to make the stadium ready for baseball. Mincher expressed concerns about the stadium being ready on time. "I'm very concerned right now, and I will be concerned until the weekend is over," Mincher said a day before the home opener.

Mark Bechtel, an editor for *Sports Illustrated* today, was a teenager who lived near Huntsville in 1985 and remembered his father taking him to games. "You could tell the city needed to build something very quick," Bechtel said. "It was the first pro baseball team in the town in fifty-five years." The Stars, meanwhile, boasting a Cactus League record of 10-7, hopped on Eastern Airlines flight No. 132 on April 10 bound for Huntsville for a team photo shoot the next day.

Huntsville Stars

"Huntsville has evolved a great deal and the Stars kind of started it. Other than the Space and Rocket Center, there really wasn't much to do in the city. There were so many different promotions to bring family and friends. Our office was temporarily placed on old airport land. We were upstairs and could walk out every day and see the progress of the stadium as it was being built. I will never forget the home opener."—CYNTHIA GILES, former ticket manager, Huntsville Stars, 2021

April 10, 1985: When pitcher Tim Belcher first peeked inside Huntsville's sparkling new Joe W. Davis Stadium before the season, the hitter-friendly dimensions frightened him. "Hey, Brad, centerfield looks short," he told manager Fischer, his former skipper in Madison. "It's definitely short." Some Huntsville pitchers worried the stadium would be the Southern League's model of Atlanta–Fulton County Stadium, dubbed a launching pad for its dinger-friendly confines. More surprises were ahead for the rest of the club. The team touched ground in Huntsville from Scottsdale at 3:47 p.m. for what was supposed to be a few days of touring the new stadium and working out before busing to Birmingham and then Columbus, Georgia, to start an eight-game road trip on April 12 to open the season.

But the field was not ready. In fact, the open house for the community scheduled on April 11 was even canceled because work needed to be completed on the stadium and the infield sod was still tender. Don Mincher didn't expect the 10,259-seat stadium to be fully completed until May or June. Starting the season on the road gave stadium workers more time before the highly anticipated home opener on April 19. Local fans were still able to meet players at D'Livery Stable, a local restaurant on South Parkway, before they left for Birmingham. Since seats were already installed, the stadium was ready enough for the club to gather behind the third base dugout for a team photo a day after arriving. During the orientation, they visited their new clubhouse and noticed new patriotic uniforms hung in their locker stalls. "Being promoted to Huntsville was huge for me," Greg Cadaret said. "We were the only A's affiliate that didn't wear green and gold. Our team colors were red, white, and blue. We went from white to black shoes." Many players were impressed with the look of Joe Davis Stadium and thought it resembled a miniature Major League stadium.

The Stars opened the season with twenty-one players on what was designated a twenty-two-man roster:

Stan Javier	Ray Thoma
Greg Cadaret	Brian Graham
Tim Belcher	Bob Hallas
Charlie O'Brien	Eric Plunk
Rob Nelson	Joe Law
Darrel Akerfelds	John Marquardt
Larry Smith	Mike Gorman
Wayne Giddings	Rocky Coyle
Jose Canseco	Terry Steinbach
Luis Polonia	Tom Zmudosky
Chip Conklin	

The late Tom Zmudosky made the club as a reliever. Like Rocky Coyle, he played for the Utica Blue Sox in 1982 before signing with Oakland. "He makes the good pitches when he has to," George Mitterwald once said of the Rome, New York, native. Growing up, the right-hander was one of eight siblings and fell in love with baseball right away. In fact, when Zmudosky's father, William, came home from work every day, he played catch with Tom while the other seven kids waited for dinner.

"He was a baseball player since he was a kid," Carmel, Zmudosky's widow, said. Playing for Rome Free Academy High School in 1978, he was 9-1 on the mound with a .390 batting average at the plate in his senior year. He was an All-Star on the basketball court, too. Tom was a quiet and reserved independent thinker with a New York edge. Ray Thoma was Zmudosky's roommate in Huntsville and remembered him as a family man who cared about others. "He was a very considerate and down-to-earth guy," Thoma said. Zmudosky later made the Rome Sports Hall of Fame in 2014, after passing away at age fifty-three in May of that year. "He knew he was going to be inducted in July, but he passed away in May," Carmel said. Zmudosky, after going 8-5 with a 3.07 earned run average for Double-A Albany in 1984, was originally slated to be on Tacoma's roster to open the season but Oakland moved him to Huntsville instead.

The Stars' ticket office, meanwhile, was booming. On March 30, the day tickets for opening night and other home games went on sale, six thousand were sold. There wasn't much interest for seats in the nondrinkers section down the first-base line. "We would like a sellout . . . would hope for a sellout," Kent Pylant, assistant general manager, said before the season, "but we're not going to predict a sellout." Cynthia Giles, the club's ticket manager at the time, remembered the rush that day. "We were constantly having foot traffic, phone calls, and fans walking up buying tickets," recalled Giles. "There was just so much excitement. So many of the skyboxes were sold to the business community. People loved baseball." Bringing Major League flavor, the San Diego Chicken was scheduled to make an appearance at Joe Davis Stadium on June 17.

Giles was a busy ticket manager and felt lucky to have landed the gig. In the summer of 1984, she had been following the roller-coaster journey of the team coming to town. The franchise soon announced a job opening for ticket manager, and she immediately mailed her resume in. "I interviewed with Larry [Schmittou], Don [Mincher] and Kent [Pylant], and they hired me right away," Giles remembered. "They were still deciding on an office manager."

The club also needed to make decisions on the broadcasting front. Like Giles, Rick Davis, a sports director at two local television stations—WAAY and WAFF—in Huntsville for over eight years, was closely monitoring Larry Schmittou's pitch to bring the franchise. When Davis learned the move was official, he pitched a move of his own to Mincher. Davis told Mincher he was interested in being the team's play-by-play broadcaster. Davis had a body of work in sports broadcasting that included calling football and basketball games for the University of North Alabama, a Division II school about seventy miles from Huntsville. "Rick was one of the top sportscasters here for a number of years," said John Pruett.

Davis never worked in baseball as a broadcaster. But the savvy, thirty-four-year-old Davis, a native of Cleveland, Tennessee, had followed the sport for many years and wanted a chance. Having grown up listening to legendary baseball broadcasters Harry Caray, Ernie Harwell, and Mel Allen by virtue of a tiny transistor radio in the late '50s and early '60s, Davis always had an itch to narrate baseball to the masses. He was fascinated by how Allen masterfully described the action. "Mel sounded as if he was right next door to my house," said Davis. "Listening to Allen describe a game at Yankee Stadium was pure magic. I fell in love with the Yankees, but more importantly with baseball. Later, when I heard Caray and Harwell, it was more evidence that baseball was amazing, and I wanted to be a part of it."

Being the radio voice of Huntsville's first professional baseball club in fifty-five years was a dream job for Davis. Davis and Mincher had crossed paths before. He had interviewed Mincher during a World Series shortly after Mincher retired from baseball after the 1972 season. After retiring, Mincher had opened a trophy shop in Huntsville. "He was incredibly gracious and patient with a young, naïve sportscaster like me," Davis said. Once Davis felt he was positioned to land the play-by-play gig in August 1984, he asked Mincher if he would serve as his color commentator. The only problem was that Mincher was on the verge of becoming the general manager. "He told me, 'Well, I'd love to do that, but I think I'm going to be the general manager,'" Davis recalled. "I figured he would be involved somehow."

But Mincher advocated for Davis and endorsed him to Schmittou. Mincher had built enough capital in Schmittou's eyes that Schmittou asked Davis for an audition tape. Davis admitted to them he couldn't present any baseball work because he had no experience broadcasting the sport. Schmittou still wanted to hear Davis in action. "So, we drove to a radio station in north Huntsville—WTAK-AM 1000 (formerly WVOV)—and I put my tape on a reel machine in one of the production studios. I identified to Larry and Don which button to push and closed the door. The tape was a clip from one of my basketball games between UNA and Troy State. They listened for about forty-five seconds, came out, thanked me, and left. A day or two later, Don called and told me I had the job. I was pumped. But even though I thought I knew baseball well; I later found out how clueless I was about the sport. And I didn't know what I didn't know. I learned over the course of the 1985 season." Davis said the learning curve of covering baseball full time was humbling. "It was like drinking water from a fire hose," he admitted. The Stars boasted a five-station radio network, led by WFIX-AM 1450, including an FM station (WFMH-FM). Randy Davidson, a Huntsville native and former Minor League second baseman in the Cincinnati Reds organization, was hired as a color commentator to compliment Davis, the club's new voice.

While the broadcasting crew was set, the team needed a place to practice before making the trek to Birmingham. They found a local mill field to hold workouts and a bunch of fans showed up to see them. "They practiced at Huntsville Park, which doesn't exist anymore," Davis remembered. "Back then, it was the closest thing to a regulation, full-sized baseball park. They held workouts there. It was a small, amateur park that was in decent shape." Rocky Coyle remembered the workouts there. "The whole town was watching us practice at some city park before the season because the field wasn't ready," he said.

As Huntsville was poised to open the season against the Barons— league champions in 1983—at Rickwood Field on April 12, Fischer rolled out the first opening day lineup in franchise history. He tapped Joe Law, twenty-three, as the starting pitcher for the Friday start. Law, a right-hander, had posted strong numbers in Modesto the previous season. He was 11-2 with a stingy 2.58 earned run average. "Joe had a good arm," said catcher Charlie O'Brien, who was behind the plate when Law pitched, "he was a good pitcher." Belcher, the flame-throwing glamour boy of Oakland's organization, was lined up to start the home opener on April 19. "Everyone wondered who the starters were going to be," Pruett said. "We had been reading Bob Mayes's reports from Arizona and Fischer played it to a hilt because he didn't want to tip Birmingham until opening night. But we explained to him that since we were an afternoon paper, the lineup would not be in print until the Stars were chartering to Birmingham. He finally gave in to us, but he didn't announce the lineup to everyone else until game day. The expectations were very high for the club."

Fischer's inaugural Stars lineup:

Luis Polonia, LF	Rocky Coyle, DH
Charlie O'Brien, C	Brian Graham, 2B
Stan Javier, CF	Ray Thoma, 3B
Jose Canseco, RF	John Marquardt, SS
Rob Nelson, 1B	Joe Law, SP

"I'd like to beat their pants off and create a rivalry that way," Mincher said of the other Alabama club. The Stars immediately showcased their power on opening night. But so did Birmingham, the Double-A club of the Detroit Tigers who finished in fourth place the previous season. Huntsville, after leading the Barons 7–6 through four innings, couldn't contain them. Birmingham erupted. Catcher Scotti Madison slammed a grand slam in the fifth to put the Barons on top 10–7 before Canseco drilled a run-scoring double and Nelson blasted a two-run homer in the top of the sixth to tie the game 10–10. But Birmingham stormed back and scored another five runs on five hits in the bottom half of the inning to retake the lead and never looked back. In a slugfest, the Barons overpowered the Stars 15–12 on seventeen hits, handing Huntsville the first loss of the season. While the club's pitching faltered badly in the first game, Nelson shined for the Stars with two home runs and three runs batted in.

Third baseman Ray Thoma remembered the strange first game of the season. "We had put so much hard work in during spring training, then we got teased in Huntsville with a new stadium and the warm people there, and then we had to open the season on the road," Thoma said. "We had one of the best Minor League stadiums in the country and had to open up in the oldest one. We knew we couldn't go undefeated the whole season and couldn't wait to play on our own field." The Stars craved some home cooking. Beginning in spring training, the players had been living out of suitcases for almost two months.

Huntsville bounced back from the opening night loss and dominated. While the Barons terrorized the Stars' pitching in the first game, the next day was a different story. Cadaret, the starter, tossed five shutout innings in game one of a doubleheader, and Plunk fired five hitless innings in the nightcap as Huntsville swept a pair 7–1 and 4–2. The Stars left Birmingham with three straight wins. Polonia and Javier ignited the top of the lineup to set the table for the thunder of Nelson and Canseco. Javier was 4 for 10 and Polonia was 6 for 16 in the opening series. "Luis was a little mosquito," said Cadaret. "He'd slap the ball and run like hell." Infielder Chip Conklin also spanked two homers for the Stars. Despite the 3-1 record to open the season, Huntsville's pitching was a surprising concern. Besides reliever Larry Smith earning two saves in the opening series, the relievers were shaky, and the pitching staff left Birmingham with an earned run average of 5.23. Stars pitchers allowed twenty-one walks in thirty-one innings. "I'm not satisfied at all," Gary Lance, the pitching coach, told Bob Mayes, a beat writer. "We're walking too many people and getting behind the hitters too often. Plus, our pitch selection hasn't been very good."

Lance hoped his staff would turn it around in Columbus, where they played the undefeated farm club of the Houston Astros, in a four-game set at Golden Park. After heavy rains wiped out the first game, the

Stars were forced to play a doubleheader for the second consecutive series, which complicated the pitching rotation. But the club was up to the challenge and swept their second doubleheader in four days, 6–2 and 9–4, against Columbus. Through only six games, Huntsville had already scored forty-five runs and smashed ten home runs, boasting a sizzling .280 batting average. "We had a lot of power, speed, and great defense," remembered Javier. "It was a great team from the beginning." Everyone was getting into the act. Javier lived on the bases and every non-pitcher on the team had at least one hit or scored one run. The explosive lineup was carrying the club. "I've never seen anything like it in my two years in pro baseball," Akerfelds said after the game. The Stars split the next two games in Columbus before heading back to Huntsville for the home opener with a 6-2 record. After playing in front of only 423 fans at Golden Park in the series finale, the Stars couldn't wait to play in front of thousands on April 19, the start of an eight-game home stand. "Boy, this city had better get ready because we really have a great team," Fischer said before the home opener.

Back in Huntsville, meanwhile, while the Stars roared through Birmingham and Columbus, Mincher and his front office staff were working around the clock to prepare the new stadium like a bride waiting for her groom. The agenda was full for Friday night's home debut at the new stadium. The stadium on Leeman Ferry Road was dedicated and named after Joe W. Davis, Huntsville's five-term mayor who fought hard to land the club. "Huntsville has evolved a great deal and the Stars kind of started it," said Cynthia Giles. "Other than the Space and Rocket Center, there really wasn't much to do in the city. There were so many different promotions to bring family and friends. Our office was temporarily placed on old airport land. We were upstairs and could walk out every day and see the progress of the stadium as it was being built. I will never forget the home opener."

The pregame festivities for the home opener, featuring fireworks and a parachute skydiver gliding into the stadium, were slated to start at 6:50 p.m., with a game time of 8:00 p.m. The ownership group of nine—Conway Twitty; Richard Sterban; Reese L. Smith Jr.; Reese L.

Smith III; Mark W. Smith; Stephen B. Smith; Walter Nipper Jr.; George Dyce; and the front man and president, Schmittou—were also scheduled to be introduced. Twitty, one of the kings of country music, declined an offer to play pro ball in 1950 after serving in the army. He batted over .400 as a centerfielder. He had recently opened "Twitty City," an entertainment club in Henderson, Tennessee. Sterban, a bass singer for the Oak Ridge Boys, was a backup singer for Elvis Presley in the 1960s. He loved baseball and aspired to be a broadcaster at one point. The Oak Ridge Boys had won a Grammy Award in 1981 for the smash hit "Elvira." "Finding out they owned the club made us feel like bad asses," Thoma said. Dyce also served as the general manager of the Nashville Sounds.

But as the excitement grew for the first pitch, the bumpy playing surface inside the stadium was a growing concern. The infield and out-field grass that was made up of fifteen thousand square yards of sod were patched together like a quilt. Heavy rain earlier in the week made it even more difficult to make the field playing ready. Even Charles Crute, Huntsville's head groundskeeper, expected unpredictable hops come game time, but he insisted the field was playable. Huntsville's infielders, though, had been worried about rocks in the infield dirt since they first arrived on April 10. "The field was so new, and the ground was still settling," remembered Thoma. Javier also noticed the grass was in poor shape. "They had just laid the grass and the ball was bouncing everywhere," he said. "But as soon as we started playing, I didn't mind. We had a great bunch of guys."

While the sod was settling on the ground, excitement was in the air for the home opener, and Belcher was taking the mound for the Stars that night. But there was anxiety at the ballpark. Stadium workers were scrambling to make it baseball ready. "The paint was still wet when we got there," said Thoma. Fischer remembered the finishing touches before opening night. "When players started arriving to play, the carpenters were packing their tools and leaving the ballpark. It came down to the wire." Rick Davis recalled workers preparing the stadium when he arrived to prep for his broadcast duties. "I remember walking down the third base concourse of the stadium on opening night and workers were hanging signs along the concourse," said Davis. "It was that close. They literally finished about 5:00 p.m."

Mark McCarter, a former columnist for the *Huntsville Times*, described the rush to ornament the stadium before opening the gates. "The last-minute work was well worth it," wrote McCarter in 2005. "They were putting on the finishing touches, like a salesman polishing a gem before it leaves the store, a tailor with the last hand-stitching on a $5,000 tux." Excited fans formed long lines in front of the stadium gate hours before first pitch. "They were cheering when we walked into the locker room," Coyle said. "The stadium was new, plush, and magical. Huntsville didn't have a Major League team, but they had us. The stadium was electric that night."

The thrilling pregame festivities validated Coyle's point. Not only was Joe Davis on hand to throw out the ceremonial first pitch, but several dignitaries, including the four city council members—Jimmy Wall, John Glenn, Bill Tallent, and Ernest Kaufmann—who passed a 4–1 vote to build the multipurpose stadium in August, attended the game. Tommy Battle, Huntsville's mayor today, had just been elected to the city council and was present. "The city council got to run on the field, and the fans clapped for us," Battle said. "We had a great time. It was a great atmosphere for the community." Baseball executives who were instrumental in bringing the pro club to Huntsville came. Besides Schmittou, Walt Jocketty, Oakland's director of baseball administration, flew in to celebrate the new partnership. Mincher, antsy and nervous to ensure everything ran smoothly, was everywhere. "This is the most exciting thing that has happened to Huntsville since man landed on the moon," Councilman Glenn said. Fischer recalled the moments before the game: "It was so new and exciting for everyone, and we had a great team," he said.

As a crowd of 10,022 crammed the newly christened Joe W. Davis Stadium, they sensed a renewed excitement not felt in the city for a long time. The attendance was remarkable considering only a total of 12,734 fans watched the Stars during their eight-game road trip through

Birmingham and Columbus to open the season. "It was jam-packed," David Sharp, a batboy for the Stars in 1985, noted. "Parking was a nightmare. Everyone wanted to be there. Even non-baseball people came to be a part of it and see the stadium." Mark Mincher, Don's son, remembered he and his brother-in-law being parking attendants at the stadium that night. He said keeping track of the cars coming in was overwhelming. "We charged two dollars to park that night, and we had such a hard time trying to get cash from people," he said. "We had so many one dollar bills flying around, I was on a golf cart trying to chase them. It was unbelievable. We worked our tails off that night. People were everywhere. It was hard to describe."

Inside the stadium, the Stars overwhelmed Birmingham and electrified the packed house. The defense set the tone in the first when Javier, playing center, made an incredible leaping catch to rob Rondal Rollin of extra bases to kill Birmingham's first inning rally. The Stars took control from there and never looked back. The patched-up outfield grass came into play right away, when Thoma drilled a line drive in the bottom of the first that took a bad hop over centerfielder Rodney Hobbs's head for an inside-the-park home run. It was already Thoma's third game-winning RBI of the season. O'Brien clubbed the first fence-clearing home run in stadium history in the second. Canseco blasted a titanic grand slam home run over the left field scoreboard to highlight a six-run explosion in the seventh. Performing for the first time in Huntsville, Canseco's prodigious power had left quite an impression on the fans. "We were at the main entrance counting money behind a berm beyond the left-field fence," remembered Mark Mincher, "and we looked up and suddenly there was a ball falling from the sky and rolling down the berm. We later found out it was Canseco's home run." Canseco soon earned the nickname "Parkway Jose" for his homers that rolled toward Memorial Parkway outside the stadium.

John Marquardt, the shortstop, collected three hits and drove in three runs, including a two-run homer in the fifth. Brian Graham also collected three hits. Belcher, meanwhile, pitched as advertised. He tossed six one-hit shutout innings before yielding to reliever Wayne Giddings, who closed the door on the Barons with three shutout innings, resulting in the Stars mauling of Birmingham 10–0. "Giddings didn't overpower a lot of guys, but he had good stuff," recalled Fischer. "He was kind of an unsuspecting type of guy who went out and pitched his tail off every night with a great sinker ball."

Fans stopped Joe Davis to thank him during the game for their new baseball team. "Mayor Davis was for the community," said Stars infielder Rick Stromer, who arrived for the home opener to complete the twenty-two-man roster. "Bringing a team to the community was big for him." To young adults, watching baseball at the new stadium gave them an alternative to frequenting bars. For many fans, it was Christmas in the spring. The Stars were another feather in the city's hat. The franchise would soon be awarded the President's Trophy for boasting the largest opening day crowd in the league. Many felt the stadium rivaled some Major League facilities. "The stadium was beautiful," said Canseco. "It was brand-spanking new, and we couldn't wait to play there. We had heard about it. The clubhouses were great, and the ballpark was well manicured and beautiful. The lights were perfect. The hitting background was so nice." Conklin shared Canseco's sentiment. "Modesto was fun, but now we're in a stadium with a maximum capacity of over ten thousand," he said. "When we got to Huntsville, we had a feeling the experience would be different with the newspaper and television coverage. We had games that were televised, and Rick Davis, our radio voice, got to know our guys well. He was a tremendous guy. The players really liked him."

The Stars sent fans home hypnotized after only one home game. "We stomped teams right out of the gate," said O'Brien. "We had an incredible team. The fans were excited, and we had a new stadium. We dominated, and I enjoyed Huntsville. The fans treated us like royalty." Giles said her ticket office was so busy for the home opener that she couldn't remember much of the game. "We were so busy," she said. "I was in the ticket office, and it was nonstop. But even though we were so busy, it was fun."

As April gave way to May, first-place Huntsville finished the first month with a record of 14-5, a .737 winning percentage, the league's top record. The club held a commanding four-and-a-half-game lead over Knoxville and Memphis—both 10-10. As the new franchise exploded from the gate, the big story was how fans were pouring inside the stadium to see them play. "The team became almost mythical even during the season," remembered Sandy Alderson, Oakland's general manager at the time. "It was important for us to keep that team together."

Through the first three home dates alone, almost twenty thousand came to see them play. Tom Squires of *The Tennessean* described the baseball revival taking over Rocket City. "The most excited baseball town in the South may be Huntsville, Alabama, where the Sounds moved their Class AA Southern League franchise. The Stars, an affiliate of the Oakland A's, are off to a sensational start both on the field and at the gate." Mincher was even impressed with Huntsville's sizzling start. "I felt it was kind of a tossup how Double-A ball would go in Huntsville," he admitted in 1985. "I had my doubts. But the more I got into it and got the fans' reaction, I had a feeling that it was going to be good." On May 5 a record crowd of 10,781 stuffed the stadium to see the Stars fall to the Jacksonville Expos 9–1 for what would be Huntsville's first official sellout of the season. The Stars swept their fifth doubleheader in five tries on May 10. They were only 10-10 in single games but 10-0 in doubleheaders.

On the field, Canseco's legend grew, and he was the league's early story. Through twenty-five games, he had hit fourteen homers and amassed forty-five runs batted in with a batting average of .346.

He was on pace to shatter the league's single-season home run record of forty-two, established by Orlando's Tim Laudner in 1981. Even opposing clubs were marketing Canseco as the league's biggest attraction. They encouraged fans to come see the next Babe Ruth. "In my forty-two years in baseball, the stretch he had was probably the most unbelievable and spectacular thing I'd ever seen," said Fischer, who also served as the third-base coach. "Every time he would come up, I would have to move as close to the outfield as I could, because if he hit a line drive foul, I might not be able to get away. He impacted the game more than anybody I'd ever seen."

But on May 13, while the club visited the Greenville Braves at Greenville Municipal Stadium, twenty-year-old right-handed fireballer Duane Ward fractured Canseco's left pinky finger with an inside fastball in the ninth, placing him on the ten-day disabled list. Canseco had been 2 for 4 in the game. "He was having the most incredible year until Ward hit him," said Cadaret. Many wondered how the club could keep winning and maintain their division lead without their best slugger in the lineup. Losing Canseco after only a month was a blow to the team and the city. The club kept playing, though, and fans kept filing in to see them.

7

The Huntsville Kid

"Coming to Huntsville and seeing Joe Davis Stadium, a big, brand-new ballpark, you got to sit down in the stands and talk for twenty minutes with Don Mincher, a guy right off your baseball cards from the 1960s. It was a wild moment for me. Anyone who collected baseball cards in the 1960s knew who he was."—**MARK MCCARTER**, former columnist, *Huntsville Times*, 2021

As a baseball player, Donald Ray Mincher never needed to worry about anything. When his name was called, he just suited up and ran on the field. When he played for the Washington Senators, Minnesota Twins, California Angels, Seattle Pilots, Texas Rangers, and Oakland A's over his thirteen-year Major League career from 1960 to 1972, he just showed up to spring training to start a new season. Back in Huntsville, Don's wife, Patsy Ann Payne, gathered their three children—Mark, Donna, and Lori—every summer and traveled to every city he played. The summer visits were the only time they were able to spend with him other than the offseason. "I had a military mindset," Patsy remembered. "Wherever he would go, we'd go. We tallied once and determined we had lived in twelve states during his baseball career."

Mark Mincher, Don's oldest child, recalled the routine and lifestyle. "Dad would go to spring training and mom stayed back and raised us," he remembered. "When school was out, mom loaded us up to go wherever dad was. When school started back up, we came back to Huntsville. It was a unique way to grow up." Raising three children, Don and Patsy taught them to treat everyone with respect and judge others by what they do, not by their appearance. They instilled a strong sense of family in them and to always take pride in everything they did. Don involved his family in everything he did. "We celebrated family birthdays at the stadium every year," Mark remembered.

Besides loving Patsy, his high school sweetheart, and children, he had three more loves: God, baseball, and Huntsville. Playing baseball, Mincher, standing at six feet three, was a left-handed first baseman with pop. Born in Huntsville on June 24, 1938, he was of German Irish Indian descent. He was raised on local sandlots and took pride in his city. Mincher was recognized as the No. 1 sandlot player in America in 1955. He was a staunch defender and supporter of the community. He loved seeing Huntsville shine and wanted to see the residents happy. If mayor Joe Davis was the city father of Huntsville, the good-natured Mincher was Mr. Baseball there. The community considered him a local hero—a legend. "He was a legend in Huntsville," said Brad Fischer, who met Mincher when he became manager of the Stars in 1984. "He was a popular name around town."

Playing for Huntsville's Butler High School, Mincher was All-State in football, starred in basketball, and an All-American first baseman in baseball. Jimmy Key, former Major League pitcher, also attended Butler High. Mincher was so talented that the University of Alabama offered him a baseball and football scholarship in 1956. "His true love was baseball," Patsy said. "He signed a grant to play baseball and football for UA a year before Bear Bryant, the football coach, got there." As popular as Mincher was as a superstar athlete at Butler High, he still needed to convince Patsy he was the one. "It was not love at first sight on my end," Patsy remembered. "He had to work for me. I can't say I liked him at first. He wasn't cocky but was very sure of himself." Patsy eventually fell for Don, and they married in 1956.

That same year, Mincher opted to pass on the free ride from UA to pursue a career in baseball. Instead, the seventeen-year-old touted first baseman signed with the Chicago White Sox and reported to Duluth-Superior of the Class C Northern League. He was later traded to the Senators in 1960 for power-hitting Roy Sievers and made his Major League debut on April 18, 1960, opening night. Twenty-one-year-old Mincher played alongside Harmon Killebrew, who played first and third for Washington. "We've scouted Mincher for some time and the reports on him were terrific," Cookie Lavagetto, Washington's manager, said after acquiring him. "I'm going to give the kid a real shot at the first base job."

When owner Calvin Griffith moved the Senators to Minnesota in 1961 and renamed the franchise the Twins as part of expansion, Mincher followed. By 1964 he was Minnesota's starting first baseman. Five of the next seven seasons playing with the Twins, Angels, Pilots, and A's, Mincher hit at least twenty home runs. He banged twenty-seven homers for Oakland in 1970 and finished with a career total of two hundred and a .249 batting average.

Mincher was a two-time All-Star: once with the Angels in 1967 and then with the Pilots in 1969. He made a World Series appearance with the Twins in 1965 and hit a homer off Dodgers starter Don Drysdale in his first at bat of Game One. Seven years later, in 1972, he won a championship with Oakland. In fact, in Game Four of the series against the Cincinnati Reds, Mincher, batting for Dick Green, banged a ninth-inning pinch single to right to drive in the tying run. Angel Mangual, the next batter, drove the winning run in with another single to win the game 3–2. Oakland beat Cincinnati in seven games to win the World Series that season. "He was an anchor on a bunch of really good teams," said Mark McCarter, who later covered him as a Minor League executive. "He was never a superstar but an All-Star."

After playing pro ball for sixteen seasons, including thirteen of them in the Majors, Mincher decided to retire after the 1972 season. He announced his retirement in December, two months after helping Oakland win a World Series. Oakland had an established first baseman in Mike Epstein, and Mincher saw the writing on the wall. Plus, the baseball lifestyle had worn him down. "The best part of being a baseball player is gone for Don Mincher," wrote Steve Jacobson of *Newsday* in October 1972. "The joy and high hopes of stardom have passed. Mostly the dregs are left, the last little bit at the bottom of the bottle."

Mincher was only thirty-four, but he was tired of traveling. Back in Huntsville, his fifteen-year-old son, Mark, a sophomore in high school, was exceling in sports. He wanted to follow what Mark was doing more closely. Mark was a standout prep quarterback. Mincher was lonely from being away from his family so much. In his final season, Mincher was traded to Oakland three days before the All-Star Game. He had only seen his family once since the trade. He missed Huntsville, too. "He was tired of playing and traveling," Mark said. "He could still play, but he was just tired of being away from home. He was a home guy. He liked to be home, where he could hunt, fish, and be with his family." Mincher's daughters, Donna and Lori, were also growing up fast. Donna was a high school freshmen and Lori was in sixth grade. "I don't feel like I've spent any time with them," Mincher said of his family while contemplating retirement. "I don't feel I've seen them grow up. I wonder if it's worth the sacrifice, the heartaches, the trouble to be away. And I'd like to spend the rest of my life with my wife."

Patsy cited additional factors persuading her husband to leave the game. He was dealing with a lot of pain. "Don was having a lot of shoulder problems and was starting to get cortisone shots," she said. "His arm and shoulders were hurting. He had enough. He was also tired of being traded around so many times at the end of his career. Plus, Mark was getting older, and he wanted to be home for him." But even after returning home and settling down, the game was pulling him back. Charlie Finley, owner of the A's, phoned him to make him an offer. The American League was introducing the designated hitter rule in 1973 and Finley wanted Mincher to be his left-handed designated hitter. The designated hitter replaced the pitcher in the batting lineup. Mincher, though, was used to playing first base and being used only as a hitter was not attractive to him. The whole notion of a player only hitting in a game was hard for him to comprehend back then. "It was a foreign deal to him," remembered Mark. "He told me Oakland wanted him to come back as a DH and asked me, 'How do you do that? I just don't think I can do that.' He had traveled all he wanted." Patsy remembered Don's reaction to Finley's offer: "You got to be kidding me." He declined.

Shortly after returning home, Mincher was presented with an opportunity he did pursue. He opened Don Mincher's All Sports Trophies, and running the business became a family affair for the next eleven years, which included surviving some challenging times. "We almost starved to death trying to live off that trophy shop," Patsy remembered. "I went back to college and hadn't worked since my kids were born and Don was playing." But business picked up at the trophy shop and it became the go-to vendor in Huntsville for awards and trophies. "He was so busy running the business," Mark said. "Whether engraving plaques or just selling trophies, we'd all help in the shop." Patsy, who ran the bookkeeping, recalled, "We were so busy. We sold so many uniforms and bowling shirts. Every kid received a trophy for just showing up. We had a bunch of high schools here and we got all their business. It was a good business."

Engraving and peddling award hardware for a living was becoming old for Mincher, forty-six, and he was itching to return to the game in some fashion. "He was getting tired of it," Patsy said. When he heard rumblings in August 1984 about Larry Schmittou relocating his franchise to Huntsville, he perked up. "Opening a trophy shop was just an opportunity that came up, but he was ready to get back in baseball because he missed it," Patsy noted. So intrigued was Mincher about being a part of Schmittou's new Huntsville club that he, Patsy, Mark, and Nancy, Mark's wife, drove to Nashville to meet with Schmittou to discuss an opportunity. He first thought about becoming the club's radio color commentator. Patsy remembered dropping him off in front of Herschel Greer Stadium for the meeting. But when he returned from the meeting, he told Patsy that Schmittou had offered him the job of general manager. "He went into the meeting with the intention of maybe being the color radio guy, but when he came out, he told me Larry had offered him the GM job," Patsy said. "He didn't give Larry an answer that day. He thought about it, but I knew he would accept it. He was ready."

Mark remembered the family visit to Nashville. "Dad just wanted something to do with the team," he said. "He didn't mention anything about trying to become the general manager. He was willing to do whatever. When they told him he was being considered for the general manager, he was a little surprised. When we drove there, he just wanted to be part of it. Riding back, he had an opportunity to be the GM, which was a big deal. He had always been around the game and missed it. He missed being around the players." Mincher accepted Schmittou's offer and sold his trophy shop. He was announced as general manager on September 8, 1984. "Schmittou had known Don, a local legend, and had the foresight to hire him," remembered John Pruett. "Don was terrific." Schmittou remembered Mincher from his days coaching and recruiting at Vanderbilt University when he visited Huntsville to evaluate baseball and football players. "I didn't know Don would be interested in the full-time job required to start a club because of his health," Schmittou recalled, "but we were fortunate he agreed to do it. He hired a very good staff." Becoming the general manager of a new club was a third career for Mincher—one that shouldered more responsibility than running a trophy shop or playing baseball. He was new to the front-office side of pro ball. It was a new world for him. "He played Major League Baseball, owned a small business, and now, here comes another career," recalled Mark. "It was surprising because he hadn't done anything like that before."

Mincher couldn't resist the opportunity. His loyalty to baseball and the city made him up for the challenge, and with his name now attached to Huntsville's newest pro franchise, he would do everything to make it a success. He assembled an office staff that temporarily worked out of the Huntsville Police Academy building. Like he ran the trophy shop, Mincher involved his family in running the club. Patsy ran payroll; Mark was the head parking attendant; and Donna and Lori helped in the ticket office. "I felt I could do the job," Mincher said in May 1985. "Having a team in my hometown for the first time excited me. I guess I never really got baseball out of my system." Mincher was no stranger to expansion teams. He began his career with Washington in 1960 and moved with the team when the franchise moved to Minnesota. Mincher, playing for the new Senators in 1971, followed the franchise to Texas in 1972, when the team moved there and was named the Texas Rangers. He was the only player to be on the Senators when they made their two moves.

There was no guarantee the Stars would be a success from the jump. It was only a vision and blueprint of a stadium. While the stadium was being constructed, since September 15, he worked hard to prepare for the season. "We worked harder in the winter strategizing for the following season than we did during the season," Patsy noted. While Mincher didn't have any input on the prospects Oakland was sending to Huntsville in 1985, he was responsible for fostering a first-class environment for them to play in and for the community to enjoy, and he did just that. Mincher's responsibilities were sometimes demanding and stressful. He stretched himself and worked fourteen to sixteen hours each day. "It was a steep learning curve," said Mark. "In his eyes, it was not a question of whether or not it was going to be a success. It was going to be successful, and he was going to do everything he could to make it successful. He put in a lot of hours before and after games. He was flying by the seat of his pants that first year, but he knew what it took to be successful. He just had to learn the ins and outs of the job."

In July 1985 Mincher shared his thoughts on his new gig and how his relationships with the community helped him land the job. "I didn't have any sort of experience with a job like this before," he said. "The owner thought it would be good publicity for the team because I've been very involved with the community." But even when he was not in the office or walking around the community, stresses and responsibility followed him. Patsy, for example, remembered when she and Don, leaving a Sunday morning church service and driving home on Memorial Parkway, saw black smoke billowing from the stadium's construction site. Several banks of newly delivered seats had caught fire. "He told me he wanted to see the progress of the stadium and what they had done that week," she said. "We saw the smoke. We found out the seats had caught on fire and were burning up. It was things like that he couldn't control, and the stress was difficult for him to handle at times. It was a stressful time for him."

Mincher, in his new role, was now responsible for monitoring weather systems approaching and was obsessed with inspecting the stadium's bathrooms to ensure they were clean before every game. "As a player, he never needed to worry about that kind of stuff," Mark said. "It was another added aspect of what he had to learn as a general manager. A part of his pregame routine was to check the bathrooms. He understood how important it was for the mothers to have clean bathrooms. If they saw a dirty bathroom, they probably weren't coming back."

Mark saw firsthand how tirelessly his father and staff worked, dedicating countless hours in the business and baseball operations. But he also noticed how the long hours caught up to his dad. "It took a physical toll on him, and wore him down at times," Mark said. "He was overworked and exhausted, but he was going to make sure it was a success." Besides running the Stars, Patsy remembered Mincher being responsible for non-baseball-related concerts at the stadium as part of his oversight. "He started having health problems," she said. "His blood pressure was going up, and he needed a break." But Mincher was doing something he loved.

Mincher was not afraid to roll up his sleeves and dirty up his hands when needed. For example, the crowd was so large for the home opener on April 19 that a huge mess was left around the stadium and parking lot after the game. Cups, napkins, wrappers, and cans were scattered everywhere. Even the cleanup crew couldn't pick everything up, but a game was scheduled the following night, and the stadium needed to be cleaned.

"The stadium was packed, and they couldn't get all the cars in," Patsy recalled. "Larry had suggested to Don how many staff were needed to clean up after the game. When the cleanup guys came and worked for maybe thirty minutes, they dropped their blowers and gave up cleaning. The mess was overwhelming. Then we looked up and saw Don and Larry pick up brooms to clean up."

Mingling with fans in the stands during games made the humble Mincher a beloved figure. Being so accessible to fans was the charm of the celebrated ambassador for Huntsville baseball. He was approachable. "Coming to Huntsville and seeing Joe Davis Stadium, a big, brand-new ballpark, you got to sit down in the stands and talk for twenty minutes with Don Mincher, a guy right off your baseball cards from the 1960s,"

McCarter said. "It was a wild moment for me. Anyone who collected baseball cards in the 1960s knew who he was."

Mark noted that Mincher enjoyed when fans and the community approached him. "He liked it," Mark said. "It was normal for our family. This was his hometown, and he knew a lot of folks. It was important to him that people approached him. Then he'd wander in the press box to do radio." Players and coaches approached Mincher on the field, too. He was a wealth of information and a resource for young managers in Oakland's organization such as Fischer and Keith Lieppman. "I loved talking ball with Don," Fischer remembered. "It was fun to sit around and talk about the game with him, his perspective, and what he saw on the field. I would quite often ask him his opinion on players. It was interesting to get his opinion. He was a very valuable guy to be around." Lieppman was a roving instructor in 1988 and traveled throughout Oakland's affiliates during the season. "I had great respect for him as a general manager and former player," said Lieppman. "In the South, he was very respected. He was great for our organization." On the field, if Mincher had a favorite player on the Stars, it was another first baseman. "He loved Rob Nelson because he was a left-handed first baseman like him," Fischer said. Chip Conklin, a Stars' infielder, remembered Mincher coming around the club. "He was such a gentleman and couldn't be any nicer," he said. For Ray Thoma, seeing Mincher fly from Huntsville to greet players in spring training left a lasting impression. "It was weird when we saw him in spring training because we weren't aware of any Minor League general managers who did that," he said. "He was the nicest, kindest, gentlest, and most sincere man I had ever met in baseball."

Tommy Battle had just joined the City Council in late 1984. He said he loved seeing Mincher, a local boy, running the show. "To see a former big leaguer who grew up in Huntsville become our general manager made a big difference," Battle said. "He was one of the humblest people you'd ever meet in your life. It gave us local flavor." But while Mincher was the face of the franchise, the Stars needed to keep winning on the field, but some doubted they could continue their torrid pace.

Falling Stars

"We didn't have Canseco and we didn't have Thoma at the time. Things weren't going good for us. We were getting our hits, but we just weren't scoring any runs. The guys didn't have the confidence they've had the last couple of weeks."—**BRAD FISCHER**, former manager, Huntsville Stars, June 1985

When Jose Canseco, the Southern League's home run and RBI leader, was shelved on the disabled list from a fractured left pinky finger on May 13, it killed Huntsville's momentum. The first-place Stars were 20-11 when he sustained the injury. Dave Wilder, an outfielder from Single-A Modesto, was called up to replace Canseco. Wilder was batting .303 with three home runs in thirty-one games for Modesto. After Huntsville split a four-game series with the Greenville Braves at Greenville Municipal Stadium on May 16, the club struggled badly into the All-Star break on June 6. Since that series, the skidding Stars, who started the season 14-5, had lost ten of twelve and fourteen of their next twenty games. The slump included an eight-game losing streak from May 17 to May 24, leaving the club only one game above .500 with a record of 22-21. When the Charlotte O's, the defending league champions, swept them in a four-game series at Crockett Park on May 20, it was the first time they had lost a series all season and left them nursing only a half-game lead over the hard-charging Chattanooga Lookouts. John Hart, who managed Charlotte that season, recalled the thrill of beating the powerful Stars. "We didn't have a prospect-laden team like Huntsville had, but we were consistently good all year long," he said.

"The Stars were the best team I had seen that year. They had more prospects that season than anyone else, but they also had great extra guys like Rocky Coyle. You just wondered if they were going to keep them all together."

But Oakland's hot prospects in Huntsville were suddenly losing more than winning. As the losses piled up, the club's lead in the Western Division evaporated. After returning home from a 2-6 road trip, wins remained hard to come by for the club. Nothing was going right for them. On the field, a bad hop struck hot-hitting shortstop John Marquardt's face during a May 21 loss. He required five stitches from a nearby hospital and was sidelined a few games. Huntsville was also impacted by injuries in other Oakland affiliates. In early May, infielder Ray Thoma was called up to Tacoma when Steve Kiefer was ailing from a sore elbow and placed on the disabled list. Oakland's Triple-A affiliate, the Tacoma Tigers, was struggling badly with a record of 8-16 and desperately needed help. Pressure was mounting to send Tacoma additional players. In fact, Stan Naccarato, Tacoma's general manager, had phoned A's officials in the middle of a game to make a plea for help. "I was there for a couple of weeks, and then told Kiefer's injury was not as bad as they had thought," Thoma said. But while Thoma was playing for Tacoma, he sustained an injury of his own. "We were playing in Las Vegas, and while I was turning a double play at second base, a runner slid in and tried to take me out," he remembered. "The brim of the runner's helmet caught the inside of my knee, and it swelled up. When I returned to Huntsville, I needed to do some rehab." Thoma returned to Huntsville's lineup on May 24.

More roster shuffling took place in late May. When Oakland designated Dan Meyer, a veteran infielder, for assignment on May 25, catcher Charlie O'Brien, twenty-four, was promoted to Oakland, skipping Tacoma. In thirty-three games with Huntsville, O'Brien batted .209 with seven homers and sixteen runs batted in. O'Brien became Oakland's third catcher behind Mike Heath and Mickey Tettleton. O'Brien's departure opened the door for catcher Brian Dorsett, who was promoted from Madison. Playing for the Muskies, Dorsett batted

.267 with eleven doubles and thirty runs batted in. After being told during spring training that he would be starting the season in Huntsville, Dorsett was happy to have finally reached Double-A. "I can't say enough about what happened here," Dorsett said of his time playing in Madison in 1985. "I was told in spring training I was going to Huntsville but being here has really helped. I've improved my consistency behind the plate, and I've been swinging the bat pretty well. I'm happy to be moving." Terry Steinbach, used primarily as a designated hitter for the Stars, was also being converted into a catcher that season. He had played for Brad Fischer in Madison in 1984. "Steiny was my third baseman in Madison," said Fischer. "Then we went to Double-A, and I suggested we try and make him a catcher. We knew he could hit. I would use him as a designated hitter every night." Additionally, two starting pitchers, Scott Whaley from Madison and Mark Bauer from Tacoma joined the limping Stars. Bauer had pitched for Oakland's Double-A club in Albany in 1984 and was 7-2 with an earned run average of 2.30. He began 1985 in Modesto and pitched well, earning a promotion directly to Tacoma early in the season. By May, after struggling in Triple-A, he was sent to Huntsville.

Despite the converting, roster shuffling, and playing at home, Huntsville kept sinking. In the standings, Chattanooga, who started the season 1-10, moved into a tie with them for first place. Two days later, on May 24, after Huntsville's eighth straight loss, the Knoxville Blue Jays, led by slugger Cecil Fielder, overtook Huntsville for second place. The once dominant Stars—now in third place—were looking up instead of down in the standings, with the fourth-place Memphis Chicks on their tail. Even playing in front of the home crowd couldn't ignite the Stars out of their slump. As Bill McCutchen of the *Huntsville News* penned on May 22, "It's like a traveling salesman who comes home from a fruitless trip, only to find his power and phone has been cut off and there's an eviction notice on the front door. And his dog has run away." In the stands, not as many fans were showing up. Only 1,603 fans came to Joe Davis Stadium on May 30 to watch Huntsville lose to Knoxville 8-2. It was Huntsville's smallest crowd of the season at the time. Although the Stars always occupied the bases with hits and scored first in most games, they couldn't come up with timely hits to score more runs. "We didn't have Canseco and we didn't have Thoma at the time," Fischer said in 1985. "Things weren't going good for us. We were getting our hits, but we just weren't scoring any runs."

The only strength keeping Huntsville hovering around .500 was the offense. As May gave way to June, the Stars were still hitting .280 without Canseco, who started taking batting practice again to prepare for his June 3 return. Steinbach had put together an eleven-game hitting streak and Luis Polonia boasted a fifteen-game hitting streak to fuel the offense. Marquardt was 13 for 26 during a stretch in late May. Rob Nelson, who also had an eight-game hitting streak, had clubbed twelve homers by June 2. Nelson was awarded the league's Player of the Week for the final week of May. Stan Javier, meanwhile, was always on base. He ended up with an on-base percentage of .419 with 112 walks and 61 stolen bases that season. Javier also dazzled in the outfield. "He could go after it," remembered Mark Bauer, who pitched in twenty-two games for the Stars. "He was probably our best defensive outfielder, especially at catching balls. He would always be ready."

But the pitching staff's 4.20 earned run average was the biggest concern, though Eric Plunk and Darrel Akerfelds both started the season 5-1. Plunk, because of his explosive fastball, was one of the league's top pitching prospects. On May 31 Belcher coughed up five earned runs against Knoxville and couldn't escape the second inning in an 11–5 loss. Belcher started the game with an earned run average of 3.66 and saw it inflate to 4.44 after the shelling. A pleasant surprise came from the bullpen. Closer Wayne "Gator" Giddings earned seven saves and posted a stingy 2.10 earned run average, the lowest on the staff, by early June. Giddings's success on the mound was remarkable considering he was not supposed to be the club's closer before the season.

In 1984, while playing in Madison, Giddings earned a spot in the starting rotation after pitching well as a long reliever. He led Madison's starting rotation with a 2.79 earned run average and six complete games. He preferred being a starting pitcher. The plan was for him to be on

Huntsville's starting rotation until Oakland acquired some pitching prospects. Giddings was the odd man out. "I was going to be the fourth or fifth starter in Huntsville, but during the winter, Jocketty sent me a contract to go back to Madison," Giddings remembered. "Puzzled, I asked him about me going to Huntsville and he said they had just picked up Jose Rijo, Tim Birtsas, Belcher, and Plunk, and I got bumped. So, it wasn't in the cards for me." But Giddings made the club as a long reliever when the season started and became Huntsville's most reliable arm out of the bullpen. "I came in during the opening series in Birmingham and got outs and came back to Huntsville and got more outs," he said. "I'm suddenly the guy coming out of the bullpen. I threw strikes and got outs. Brad had comfort in me because he was my manager in Madison a year before. My role wasn't really defined until midway through the season. I don't think I ever got a chance to learn to be a closer. I was just learning it day by day. I was just happy to get in a game."

Despite Giddings's late-inning heroics, by June 1, the Stars had dropped to 25-26. The club was below .500 for the first time since their opening day loss to Birmingham on April 12. Huntsville's mysterious pitching problems continued, and Bill Mooneyham, a stingy, righty reliever from Modesto, joined the club to help. The California Angels released Mooneyham in the spring and Oakland picked him up and sent him to Modesto. He was 2-0 with a 1.26 ERA for Modesto before the promotion.

Reliever Tom Zmudosky was one of the casualties of the club's dive and shakeup. He was released in late May and later joined Birmingham's staff. Zmudosky's widow, Carmel, recalled when her late husband was told he was being released. "He came inside the car and was just staring out of the window," she said. "He looked at me and said, 'I think we're going to have to go home.' I didn't know what he meant by that. The baseball world was new to me. He said they were reorganizing the team and he was released." But he wasn't quite ready to end his career and didn't go home. "He told me he wanted to give it one more shot, so we drove to Birmingham," Carmel said. After finishing the season with Birmingham, he retired and became a successful executive in the car industry.

The rotation was also impacted by injuries, and some of the players battled change. Akerfelds was sidelined with right arm soreness for several weeks and Greg Cadaret, another starting pitcher, said his troubles coincided with Oakland trying to tinker with his pitching delivery after he pitched well early on. After posting a record of 13-8 with a 3.05 earned run average in 171 innings with Modesto the previous season, he was moving up in the A's system. And off the field, Cadaret started a family. He married his girlfriend, Debbie, during the offseason and couldn't wait to pitch in Huntsville. "It started out good until the organization decided they wanted to change my windup mechanics," said Cadaret. "John Tudor, another lefty starter, had a big year and they wanted me to suddenly throw like him. He was a soft-throwing lefthander who threw around the ball and I couldn't do it." The twenty-three-year-old Cadaret was losing velocity on his fastball and forfeited control because of the change. Opposing hitters now had the advantage of seeing the ball leaving his hand earlier. He usually threw the ball over the top, but now he was throwing with a sweeping motion. "I was 3-0 when they asked me to make that change," he said. "After losing seven straight games, I was back in Modesto." The experiment proved to be a mistake. He was 3-7 with a 6.00 ERA when he was demoted to Modesto in July. After having his most challenging season in the A's system in 1985, Cadaret eventually reached the big leagues with Oakland as a reliever in 1987 and had a ten-year career with eight teams.

To make room for Canseco's return on June 3, the Stars lost a spark-plug. Madison hit a rough stretch and desperately needed hitting, and the scrappy and popular Rocky Coyle, a fan favorite in Huntsville, was the one sent there. "We're going to need some help and quickly," Jim Nettles, Madison's manager said at the time. "We haven't been hitting the ball very well." Madison had lost seven of ten. Losing Coyle didn't sit well with Huntsville fans. He was popular in the community and at twenty-five years old, was like an older brother to many of his teammates. Thousands of fans rebelled against the move and even signed a petition to keep him in Huntsville, but only Oakland decided on Minor League assignments. The community presented the petition to Coyle before he drove to Madison with his family. He was hitting .265 for the Stars. "To this day, I don't know why I was demoted," Coyle recalled. "They never told me, but I had a family and had to drive from Huntsville to Madison. I was a California League All-Star in 1984 and now I'm suddenly in Madison with a fish on my jersey. When I arrived there, Nettles, the manager, pulled me into his office and told me he didn't know why I was there, but he was going to get me back as fast as he could. He helped me through the sadness of it. I was a father and a husband. We couldn't afford a place in Madison, so my wife had to live with her mom in New Jersey." Playing left field, Coyle immediately ignited Madison's lineup when he arrived. He batted .333 with an on-base percentage of .444 in twenty-four games in the Midwest League.

Back in the Southern League, the Stars kept struggling. As Huntsville battled through the difficult, three-week stretch, there was finally some promising news: three players on the Stars—Canseco, Plunk, and Akerfelds—were named Southern League All-Stars. They were voted in by the league's ten managers and beat reporters. After missing twenty-three games from injury, Canseco was still the only unanimous choice. He led the league with a .352 batting average, fifteen home runs, and fifty runs batted in. Canseco donned jersey No. 44 in honor of his favorite player—prolific slugger Reggie Jackson. "I like Reggie Jackson," Canseco told the *Huntsville News* after his All-Star selection. "He has awesome power. He's very impressive. He's got that home-run style. I'm a power hitter that makes things happen. My offensive hitting is what's going to get me into the big leagues, even though I have a good arm." Plunk was 6-2 with a 3.23 earned run average, and Akerfelds, 5-3 with a 3.77 ERA, but he was 5-1 before his last two starts.

The All-Stars played the National League's Houston Astros in the Southern League's forty-fifth annual All-Star Game. Canseco, Akerfelds, and Plunk were excited about playing a Major League team for the first time. The game was held at Birmingham's Rickwood Field on June 6.

The league also celebrated Rickwood Field's seventy-fifth anniversary. John Hart, who led the Charlotte O's to a league championship in 1984, managed the All-Stars against the Astros. But Houston silenced them 3–0 in the game. Canseco, who batted cleanup and played right field, was 0 for 2, and Plunk, coming out of the pen, tossed two innings. Akerfelds never made an appearance in the game.

Although Huntsville won their final two games against the Memphis Chicks before the All-Star Break, pushing their record to 28-27, division-leading Chattanooga beat them two straight games when they returned home on June 7. The fourth-place Stars fell to 28-29 in the tight four-team division race. The club showed frustration during the June 7 game at home. With the Stars trailing 5–0 in the fourth inning, home plate umpire Paul Terry ejected a fuming Canseco over arguing a strike call. Canseco, who had been called out on a third strike in his first at bat, felt the pitch was too outside. When he was ejected, Fischer charged from the dugout to confront Terry. Fischer faced off with Terry, and the umpire ejected him, too. Fischer kicked dirt and threw his cap in disgust. Pitching coach Gary Lance replaced Fischer and Wilder replaced Canseco in right for the remainder of the game. The frustrating home losses gave Huntsville a disappointing home record of 12-18. After starting the season 14-5 and leading the division by five games at one point, Huntsville was 14-24 over the next thirty-eight games. With only fourteen games left in the first half, the Stars were on the verge of an embarrassing collapse. A lot was at stake in the final games of the first half. The first half winners of the league's Western and Eastern Division would automatically clinch a playoff berth. The next two weeks would reveal whether the Stars would be good enough to overcome adversity or be a talent-laden bust.

Huntsville Lumber

"When you sat inside Joe Davis Stadium and looked toward centerfield, you could see a sign that read 'Huntsville Lumber Company' down the highway. I thought to myself, 'How appropriate for this team' because we had some lumber in our lineup. It was an unbelievable team."—**WALT JOCKETTY,** former A's director of baseball administration, November 2020

After starting the season with a disappointing home record of 12-18, it was only fitting the fourth-place Stars caught fire on the road before it was too late. Being only three games behind first-place Chattanooga with fourteen games left in the first half was encouraging for Huntsville, considering how poorly they played at home. More reason for optimism was that they were scheduled to play Chattanooga, Memphis, and Knoxville—the three clubs ahead of them in the standings—in the final two weeks of the half. And what better place to start a winning run than playing the Lookouts on the road at Chattanooga's Joe Engel Stadium, especially with a healthy Canseco and Akerfelds returning. There, the Stars won two in a row before returning home to face the Charlotte O's in a four-game series on June 11. Playing John Hart's club was a measuring stick for clubs. The O's were tough to beat and had swept Huntsville in a four-game series at Crockett Park in May.

Back home, Huntsville strutted game-swaying power in back-to-back fashion against Charlotte on two swings. On June 12, after trailing Charlotte 3–0 in the third, Canseco launched a three-run bomb toward Memorial Parkway in left to tie the game and Rob Nelson followed with a solo homer to right to take a 4–3 lead. In front of a crowd of 7,871, the Stars beat the O's 6–4 for their fourth straight victory. Brad Fischer stressed the importance of winning at home after the game. "Winning on the road is great, but when you can start winning back at home, that really picks up the team's spirits," he said. "Tonight was a big win that we really needed. We decided that our only problem was ourselves, and we seemed to have overcome it, so hopefully we can get back to the business at hand—winning."

The Stars granted Fischer's wishes the following game when they won their fifth straight. This time, Stan Javier's clutch two-out single in the bottom of the eighth gave the Stars a 3–2 victory over Charlotte and sole possession of first place for the first time since May 22, with nine games left in the first half. Chattanooga and Knoxville had lost. "Beating Charlotte was always a delight because they always fielded a strong team," Fischer said. Another encouraging sign was that Akerfelds pitched seven strong innings in the contest, the most since coming off his three-week stint on the disabled list with a sore shoulder. The club had come to life at the perfect time, and their resurgence was no surprise to the skipper in the opposing dugout. "The minute I saw that club, I was impressed," recalled Hart. "They were the best group of prospects in the league. Oakland was developing them, and Fischer ran a good program for his guys. Canseco stood out and Nelson had a big year. I loved Javier and thought Polonia had a chance to be a Major League leadoff guy. Steinbach was a winning player. They pitched well and I knew guys in that rotation had a chance to pitch in the big leagues. I liked Akerfelds, Plunk, and Cadaret. Belcher was competitive and had good stuff. I knew he would be a good Major League starter in a couple of years. They threw good arms at you all the time. Their bullpen had good pitchers. Plus, they were well managed."

After sweeping Charlotte, Huntsville wasn't finished. The red-hot Stars returned to the road on June 15 and erupted for twenty hits in Memphis against the Chicks and beat them 13–4. Canseco clubbed his eighteenth homer, and Nelson hit number sixteen. After the game, Tommy Jones, the Chicks' manager, called Canseco and Nelson "the best number three and four hitters in the league." Some critics started calling the Stars "showboats" because of their talent and dominance. "No other club in this league comes close to having as many Major League prospects as this club has," Jones said. Huntsville won seven straight games until Memphis beat them 5–1 at Tim McCarver Stadium the following day to cool them off. As hot as the Stars were, they only led Knoxville and Chattanooga by a game in the standings on June 18 with a week left in the first half division race.

While the Stars were electrifying the home crowd on the field, in the front office, Don Mincher and his staff scheduled several promotions to entertain fans. One of the popular promotions that season was a visit from the entertaining San Diego Chicken, a comic mascot, on June 17, a Monday night, against Memphis. Before the outrageous mascot began his comic musings on the field, reliever Wayne Giddings remembered when he first arrived in the Stars' locker room to suit up. "When he opened the suit box, you can only imagine the aroma that came from the chicken suit," Giddings said. "The chicken suit smelled like an entire chicken coop." During the game, Javier drove in four runs and infielder Rick Stromer extended his hitting streak to eight games with two hits to fuel the Stars to a 11–4 win. While Huntsville's clever promotions lured in some fans, the Stars' explosive lineup kept them filing in. By July Huntsville led the league in attendance and ranked fourth in the Minor Leagues, averaging 4,700 a game, behind only three Triple-A clubs: the Louisville Redbirds, Columbus Clippers, and Las Vegas Stars, in that order. Huntsville had drawn 163,000 of the league's total attendance of 470,000. The Stars were even outdrawing Larry Schmittou's new Triple-A Nashville Sounds. "The city took pride in us," Stromer said. "Seeing a packed stadium excited us. The Southern League did not have that kind of draw. Columbus drew pretty good, but no one in the league drew like Huntsville. Oakland brought Huntsville a great team right off the bat."

Walt Jocketty, Oakland's director of baseball administration, came to watch Huntsville's thunder during the season. He quickly noticed that his farm club was a perfect fit for the city. "When you sat inside

Joe Davis Stadium and looked toward centerfield, you could see a sign that read 'Huntsville Lumber Company' down the highway," he remembered. "I thought to myself, 'How appropriate for this team,' because we had some lumber in our lineup. It was an unbelievable team. We hit a lot of home runs." The lumber company joined the celebration. The staff there listened to games on the radio and whenever a player on the Stars hit a home run, they flashed their outside lights on and off.

Fischer shared Jocketty's sentiments. He knew his club was stacked with talent and even warned Mincher about the players coming Huntsville's way before the season. "I told him he may never ever see a team in Huntsville like that one," Fischer said. "I still talk about those players. They were the standard for me. They were the kind of high-quality players and character guys you could build an organization on. They were a lot of fun to be around and impacted the game in special ways."

Major League scouts marveled at Fischer's club when they moved around the league evaluating prospects during the season. George Digby, a respected scout from the Boston Red Sox, warned the rest of baseball about Oakland's Double-A prospects. He knew many of them would eventually reach Oakland and impact the American League. He told Peter Gammons of the *Boston Globe*, "Oakland is going to be a team to watch the next couple of years. That Huntsville team is one of the best Double-A clubs I've seen in a few years." Giddings concurred with Digby. "That club could have been the best Minor League team ever assembled," he said. "If you look back at how many of those players made it to the big leagues and won championships, it's impressive." Bauer joined Huntsville in May and was impressed. When he toed the rubber and looked behind him, he noticed a talented outfield. "I turned around and looked in the outfield and saw Javier in center, Polonia in left and Canseco in right," he said. "I said to myself, 'Oh my goodness.' We had good players that worked hard. There was a lot of competition, so you tried to be on top of your game. We had good starting pitchers and good relievers. We had guys who knew how to take strikes. We were fast at the top of the order. They would get on base, and we had quite a bit of power to drive them in. We had guys who were versatile and could play other positions. Our coaches were really good, too."

Ray Thoma noted the confidence and talent on the club. Although the club played with swagger, he never felt they were arrogant from the attention they garnered. Everyone was peaking at the perfect time. "Every single guy in our lineup was in midseason form and we took it out on opposing clubs," Thoma said. "We expected to win every game and never thought we would lose. We were that good. We didn't think any other team had the talent we had. We had the who's who of Minor League Baseball. I don't think there's ever been a Minor League team with that much star power and future Major Leaguers as that one. It was almost too good to be true." John Pruett, sports editor for the *Huntsville Times*, said the expectations were high because of so many young stars on the club. "We knew we were getting a lot of Oakland's young talent, and the expectation was that they were going to have a winning baseball team right away and they did," Pruett noted. "There was a lot of excitement in town, and it continued pretty much for several years after that."

Considering Oakland's Triple-A club in Tacoma, 30-40, was struggling so badly, some felt the organization intentionally loaded Huntsville with top prospects to ensure their new partnership with the city was a success right away. The notion was that Oakland wanted to bring Huntsville as many prospects as possible to make them a winning and marketable club at the expense of other affiliates like Tacoma. "If the Oakland A's Class AA farm club at Huntsville, Ala., can be considered the family's favorite son, the Class AAA Tacoma Tigers can easily qualify as the black sheep," wrote Frankie Garland of the *Modesto Bee* in June 1985.

Brian Dorsett insisted, however, the club was not only made up of prospects. "They definitely wanted to make sure Huntsville was successful, but I don't think they intentionally stacked the club," said Dorsett. "We had a lot of fill-in players, too. Not everyone in the Minors is considered a prospect. We had a combination of both." Tim Belcher, in fact, insisted some of the club's role players were inspirational and motivating. They kept everyone focused. "We had some great role play-ers on the team, too," said Belcher. "Thoma was an extra infielder and Coyle was the heartbeat of the team. They weren't big prospects, but they were the heart and soul of our team. They were hard-nosed, go-after-it kind of players that gave us an identity and kept us in check."

Rick Davis, the radio voice of the Stars in 1985, didn't think Oakland sinisterly planted their top prospects in Huntsville for any agenda other than development. "I don't think they did," Davis said. "After talking with Oakland sources, those prospects were supposed to be here at that time. The pieces were falling into place at exactly the right time." It made sense. Most of the roster was composed of players from either Single-A Modesto or Madison and were on course to promote to Dou-ble-A that season. A few of them already had a taste of Double-A Albany in 1984. Javier, who came with Plunk from the Yankees in the Rickey Henderson trade in December, was the only one on the club with any Major League experience. He played in seven games for the Yankees in 1984. Belcher came to Oakland by way of the shrewd maneuvering of Sandy Alderson, the A's general manager. Alderson shocked baseball when he plucked Belcher from the Yankees from a pool of unprotected players in the free agent compensation draft in February 1984. Javier, Plunk, and Belcher had all belonged to New York at one point before joining Oakland. Akerfelds, Seattle's first-round draft pick in 1983, came to Oakland with closer Bill Caudill in a trade for reliever Dave Beard and catcher Bob Kearney in the winter of that year.

Charlie O'Brien only played in Huntsville until he was promoted to Oakland in late May. But during his brief time there, he figured out quickly that Oakland's Double-A hub was the organization's focus. "There's no doubt that Oakland wanted to make Huntsville their shin-ing club for the season," said O'Brien. "A lot of those guys could have been pushing a big league club, and they were playing in Double-A." Plus, Huntsville landed Fischer, one of Minor League Baseball's best managers and a rising leader in the A's system.

Some insiders attributed Huntsville's loaded team to the timing of Oakland's draft picks in the early 1980s—led by the late Dick Wiencek, the scouting director. Under Wiencek's watch, Oakland drafted several players on the Stars: Canseco, Nelson, Steinbach, Cadaret, Dorsett, Thoma, O'Brien, Bauer, Marquardt, Graham, Ashman, Larry Smith, Scott Whaley, Brian Guinn, Bob Hallas, Pete Kendrick, and Todd Burns. "Our draft was really good for a couple of years and a lot of those players were rising in our system at the time," Fischer said. "Playing Double-A was just a normal step in their progression." Oakland drafted Steinbach from the University of Minnesota in 1983, and he experienced the rise firsthand. He was a part of a group of players coming up in Oakland's system and joined them in Scottsdale every spring. "For most of us, it was our third year together in the A's system," Steinbach said. "We weren't always on the same team, but we gathered in spring training every year with the same nucleus of players. Having that much talent on the club wasn't jaw-dropping to us. It was our group for our era."

Huntsville benefited from the timing and rise. As a teenager, Mark Bechtel came with his father to watch the Stars play, and the club's success made a lasting impression on him. The excitement surrounding the Stars—along with watching the talented prospects—hypnotized him. "They were an incredible team and there was a lot of excitement early in the year, partly because it was a new thing and partly because of how good they were playing," Bechtel recalled. "The people in Huntsville had to feel a little spoiled because of how good the team was. There were a bunch of guys on the team destined to make it. My dad and I thought Ray Thoma looked like a Major League player."

Rick Stromer, who played some third base for the Stars, batted cleanup for the Double-A Waterbury Angels in 1984 and was an All-Star in the Eastern League that season. His role in Huntsville's lineup in 1985 was another story. "I batted ninth on this roster, and I was proud to do it," Stromer said. "The only problem was that I became a pin cushion. I was never hit a lot, but in that lineup, opposing pitchers became frustrated and tended to take it out on the bottom of the order. But I also saw a lot more fastballs batting ninth, which was better."

Canseco, twenty, was Huntsville's can't-miss prospect who garnered the most attention for his prodigious home runs that dented light towers and peppered streets well beyond the fences. Besides basking in his own personal achievements that season, he recognized the talent on his club. Playing in Huntsville was a turning point in his career, Canseco maintained. "We had an All-Star team," he said. "The A's sent their most talented prospects to Huntsville. Look at our roster. Our starting pitching staff all became Major Leaguers. It showed the talent we had. We were winning and having a lot of fun. It was an amazing time for Huntsville and an amazing time for baseball." The rest of baseball was taking note of the city's baseball renaissance. Newspapers around the country and baseball periodicals descended on Joe Davis Stadium. "They got more publicity than any Double-A team in the country," Bob Mayes, the Stars' first beat writer, said in 2007. "I was writing a game story and sidebar every day. Our sports editor wrote columns on them. The team was not being sold short on publicity."

Being on the front page wasn't enough, though. The Stars needed to harness all the talent into a championship, which would solidify their legacy as a special club. Huntsville moved closer to a championship on June 20, having a chance to clinch the Western Division with a win over Knoxville at Bill Meyer Stadium on a Thursday evening with All-Star ace Eric Plunk on the mound. Plunk was 8-2, and Knoxville was division champion of the first half of the previous season. The four-game series with Knoxville was the final series of the first half. The Stars, 38-30, were positioned to clinch a playoff berth behind the muscle of Nelson and pitching arm of Greg Cadaret the night before. Nelson clubbed his eighteenth home run, a two-run shot, in the first, and Cadaret pitched six strong innings to carry the Stars to a 4–3 win over Knoxville to open the series. The win was the club's tenth in their last eleven games. They now held a commanding three-game lead over Chattanooga and Knoxville with three games left. Huntsville needed to win just one of their final three games against Knoxville to clinch the division.

The Stars wasted no time to record the win and secure a playoff spot in front of a crowd of 912. Even though Plunk was knocked around early, they came back in dramatic fashion, a habit that highlighted their torrid 10-1 run that started on June 9. With Huntsville down 5–3 in the top of the ninth, Canseco strolled to the plate with Polonia on second and Javier on first. He faced touted nineteen-year-old closer Luis Aquino. Aquino dominated in relief for Knoxville, and many had compared him to pitching great Luis Tiant. Aquino was considered one of the best pitching prospects in the league. The right-hander was Fireman of the Year in the Single-A Carolina League the previous season. The matchup between two of the league's top prospects was intriguing theater. Jimmy Bragan, the league's president, was on hand to watch the drama unfold. Canseco was mired in a slump and having a miserable game, striking out in his first four at bats. Instead of replacing the struggling Canseco with a pinch hitter or making him bunt the runners over, Fischer let him swing away. Earlier in the game, in the seventh inning, Canseco blasted a ball onto the roof of the Standard Knitting Mills building in left that barely hooked foul.

When Aquino released a fastball in the ninth, Canseco left no doubts. He crushed a three-run bomb to center that was estimated at over 425 feet. The mammoth blast put Huntsville on top 6–5 for good as Giddings wiggled out of a two-on, two-out rally in the bottom of the ninth to secure his eleventh save. "He was never an overpowering guy, but he threw that sinker and got grounders all the time," Fischer said of Giddings. "He was always in the strike zone and effective. He was very calm and laid-back." The Stars, in their first year of existence, were Western Division champions of the first half. Huntsville players sprayed champagne on each other and celebrated. "I'm thrilled to death," Fischer said after the game. "There aren't many times a game ends like that." The club's thirty-ninth win made the remaining two games of the first half irrelevant in the standings.

Huntsville finished the first half with a 39-32 record, winning eleven of their final fourteen games. Regardless of the outcome in the second half, Huntsville earned a spot in the playoffs in September. The Stars would either be facing the division winner of the second half in the playoffs or—if they won the second half, too—the club with the best overall record of both halves. "We are the newest team in the Southern League and we just proved that we have the talent to win the big games, so there is going to be pressure on us to win the second half too," Fischer said. "I think we can do it, but it will have to be one game at a time." The only thing set in stone was playoff baseball coming to Huntsville on the shoulders of an exciting new team with a spectacular new stadium, the gemstone of the league. The city celebrated.

10

Southern Comfort

"Huntsville rolled out the red carpet for us. It felt like we were rock stars. They literally gave us the key to the city. We felt like the city was our family. It was as if the community was waiting for their long-lost son to come back home, and they got a whole team of them. The city went from zero to one hundred miles an hour in one summer."—**RAY THOMA**, former third baseman, Huntsville Stars, 2021

Rick Stromer was not on Huntsville's opening day roster in Birmingham, but a week into the 1985 season, the third baseman not only joined the Stars, he served as the club's carpenter. The California Angels had released the twenty-five-year-old during spring training and Karl Kuehl asked him if he was interested in trying out for Oakland before they broke camp. Stromer impressed Kuehl enough during an extended spring training to join the Stars during the season-opening series on the road. The free-spirited Stromer landed the final spot on the twenty-two-man roster. He was not even on hand for the team photo at Joe Davis Stadium on April 10. "It took some time to acclimate myself there and get some playing time," he remembered. In fact, Stromer didn't appear in a game until April 24, but the club kept him busy with other duties. A carpenter by trade, Stromer was used to enhance the new stadium. For a few bucks on the side, he strapped on his tool belt after games and built cabinets for the team's second-floor offices. "I'd go up there with my tools and start on my carpentry and cabinetry work," he said.

Stromer made the most of more opportunity. While some of his teammates rented apartments and stayed with host families around town during the season, Stromer found a premier place to stay when he met Charles Crute, the club's head groundskeeper. Crute arranged for him to stay at a small executive eighteen-hole golf course his family owned less than a mile from the ballpark. Crute's family had closed the golf course. There, on the fifteen-acre property, Crute lived in an upstairs clubhouse and Stromer lived in the restaurant below. The amenities suited his lifestyle perfectly. "I was the luckiest of all of them," Stromer said. "I had a waterbed and big-screen television. I didn't have to pay any rent and had full access to the entire property that included eight televisions. I was able to work and still play golf. When it came down to deciding on something to do after hours, the team probably chose my place." Teammate Chip Conklin said Stromer partied like a rock star. "Ricky was always the last one to come home from a night of fun," Conklin said. "I used to joke that he was the only guy who could go out, have fun, and bring the band home to party with him. He was a great guy."

Stromer was one of the many players on the Stars the city welcomed and embraced. As Huntsville was growing dramatically in technology and at the forefront of the space industry in the 1980s, it lacked a sports franchise for the community to pull for, one that brought them together like other cities. The city was missing a major attraction to unite and inspire; a fascination that could bring family and friends together to enjoy. The city's craving for entertainment was evident when the Stars came to town and filled the void. Huntsville was smitten with its new obsession: Minor League Baseball. Parents brought their children to the ballpark and friends met for beer and fun there. Families of the hard-working front office staff practically lived at the stadium. "They hadn't had summer entertainment before us," Ray Thoma said. "Redstone Arsenal did only so much for them. We'd go to restaurants and fans wanted to cover our meal and asked if we needed anything else. Families invited us to their homes for dinner. They'd bring us food at the park. We'd return from a playoff game, and fans waited for us at the stadium. It was a movie."

Tim Belcher said it was a perfect romance between team and city. "It was the first time Huntsville had a Minor League franchise, and they were trying to do it right," he said. "They built a nice ballpark with some nice promotions, and Jocketty and Kuehl did right by them by sending a good roster." Players made themselves at home as they navigated the city. Stan Javier remembered he and Luis Polonia buying an old, rusty car for $250 just to get around. The vehicle was so old and running so poorly, they were begging anyone to take it off their hands. The car, you see, never turned off, and they only needed to use the brakes to drive it. "We never had to touch the accelerator because the car was always running," chuckled Javier. "It was so old. We left the car in the stadium's parking lot when we went on a road trip hoping someone would steal it. We put stickers all over it. When we got back, the car was still there. Nobody wanted it." Dave Tolbert, a season ticket holder, remembered when they purchased the car. "It was the same model Andy Griffith drove, with a yellow light on top," Tolbert said. "They pulled up to the ballpark with a yellow caution light going in circles. It was a piece of junk. I think they just left the car when the season was over."

After games, some players visited a local Irish bar, Finnegan's Pub, on Memorial Parkway, to play darts, and A&W Root Beer on Drake Avenue. Players piled into a teammate's car. A few players borrowed an older pickup truck from a fan to get around. Canseco drove his Camaro all over town. Coming to Huntsville made him a superstar. "We were celebrities everywhere we went," Canseco said. "The fans treated us with so much respect. They were never down on the team and always supported us. You had a brand-new ballpark and a winning team. It was an awesome combination. To them, we were a Major League club."

The fans treated the club like stars. Along with dominating on the diamond, the affection the community showered on the Stars made them the Beatles of Huntsville. They opened Little League ceremonies and signed autographs everywhere. "Huntsville rolled out the red carpet for us," Thoma said. "It felt like we were rock stars. They literally gave us the key to the city. We felt like the city was our family. It was as if the community was waiting for their long-lost son to come back home, and they got a whole team of them. The city went from zero to one hundred miles an hour in one summer." The players were media darlings and received strong coverage and publicity. "It was our first dose of the big leagues," said Conklin. "After games, we're on the local news." Even David Sharp, one of Huntsville's batboys, felt the celebrity. "We felt like we were a big deal," he said. "Our friends were watching us from the stands. It was neat."

The players were recognized in supermarkets and many families invited them over for some southern cooking. Joe Mays, a local rocket engineer, was one of the fans who befriended Huntsville players. "He was a wonderful older man who used to sit with his wife in the stands about three feet from our on-deck circle, and he always made a point to say hello to us," said Conklin. "He invited a few of us to his house and he made homemade biscuits, sausage, and gravy. It was delicious and we enjoyed it. The hospitality we were shown in Huntsville was incredible." Fans seated behind Huntsville's bullpen even brought peanuts for the relievers. Greg Cadaret, an avid fisherman, noted that fans took him to a fishing hole whenever he felt the craving.

Sharp said the club's early season success made it easy for the city to ride the wave and follow them. Although the Stars were not a Major League club, fans never cared. The baseball awakening happening in Huntsville transcended any pro sports league. As far as the city was concerned, the Stars were the Detroit Tigers, baseball's world champions in 1984. "It was something the city needed," said Sharp. "We didn't have anything like that before. The Stars jumpstarted the Minor League sports scene in Huntsville. They were the table-setters." Terry Steinbach said the club walked into ideal circumstances of the freshness of a city welcoming a new team. In contrast, some established Minor League teams may not have been able to muster the same fanfare as a city enthusiastic about a new toy. "The town and businesses were behind us," Steinbach said. "When we'd go places, everyone recognized us. Some players never experienced that in the Minor Leagues, so we were blessed to have had that experience." Stromer had played in the

Minor Leagues since 1981 before coming to Huntsville. He said none of those cities came close to matching the drawing power of Huntsville. "We were lucky to get 1,000 fans in some cities, and playing in the Midwest, lucky to get 200 to 300, but Huntsville was packing the stadium with 5,500 to 6,000 every night," he said.

Dave Tolbert's son, Damon, was one of those swayed boys showing up every night to watch the Stars. Dave and his wife, Carol, sat in the first row behind Huntsville's dugout and brought the eleven-year-old to every game. Damon was thrilled to see the players walking by so close. The family was obsessed with the Stars and Damon grew up in the stadium. He kissed a girl for the first time there. The Stars changed his life. If he couldn't make a road game, he'd listen to it on the radio. He read the newspaper every morning to satisfy his craving and reviewed box scores from the night before. After school, Damon worked on homework and then joined his friends at the ballpark. Watching the Stars was the prime after-school activity for many kids. They came to the ballpark early to chase foul balls and autographs. It kept them engaged in a city with limited outlets for kids to gather. "Growing up, we'd go roller skating and play outside, but we didn't have anything like the Stars," Damon said. "It was the biggest thing I had ever been around at the time. They changed everything. We did everything we needed to get to the ballpark. It gave me something to look forward to every day." Opposing teams began calling Huntsville "The Show" because they had the best players, fans, and stadium.

Damon believed the timing of the Stars arrival fueled the club's popularity more than the talented roster. The deeper narrative was that the city was ripe for a new attraction. "The talent wasn't the big draw," he said. "None of us really knew who the players were. Most of us probably never knew where the A's Class A affiliate was. It was a story of a town needing a sports venue for fans to explode in. It was an explosion of all the right things happening at the right time. It was accepted by everyone."

The Tolbert family also networked with the Stars in the community. Dave was part-owner of a local property management company. He'd build, sell, and manage property. One of Dave's properties, Hunters Ridge, was the closest apartment complex to the stadium. He rented rooms out to several players to help them get situated. "They filled fifteen of my apartments," Tolbert said. "They needed a place to live, and I provided that. We treated them well." Tolbert became acquainted with several players. He remembered driving Canseco and Steinbach one day to a local drive-thru bank. They were both seated on the front row of Tolbert's truck on the trip. They passed their paychecks to him to insert into the teller's window. He saw the figures. "I was shocked by the small amount of money on the paychecks," Tolbert said. "That's when I realized some of them needed more help. They just didn't make much money. It struck home how much those guys were sacrificing to get to the big leagues." He took Plunk, a fishing fanatic, to a local stocked fishing pond. "We'd throw our hook out there and catch a fish every fifteen seconds," Tolbert said. He recalled what the Stars meant to the community. "This was our first shot with a professional sports franchise," he said. "It was something different to do." He also noted the impression the Stars left on starstruck kids. "I don't think they realized the impact they had on the community, especially with little leaguers," he said. "You'd see the thirty kids chasing foul balls at the game. It kept my kids out of trouble."

The warmth from the community was a refreshing distraction from dealing with the sweltering heat and humid and muggy weather conditions of the South. Some of the Stars played in chilly conditions in Madison and Albany in 1984 that forced some snow outs. The travel presented more discomfort. "The weather and travel in the Southern League wears on you," Rocky Coyle said. "You're hot on a bus and away from your family." None of the cities were close to each other. To play road games, they endured long four to ten-hour bus rides on some of Conway Twitty's old tour fleet. "It was a rundown piece of junk," Brad Fischer said of one of the tour buses. The bus featured six beds in the back, and the seating was seniority-based for the players. The most tenured players usually chose the beds, especially for all-night trips. The problem was the engine below the beds made the back section of the bus hot. The breeze from the air conditioner rarely reached the end of the bus. But on shorter trips, some of them found it more comfortable to sit in the front. "When we were on shorter trips to Memphis, Birmingham, and Chattanooga, they were sweating their asses off in the back," said Cadaret. "They suddenly wanted to sit with us. But we told them, 'You picked your seat, get your asses in your bed.'"

The Stars spent most of their time traveling through the ten-city league. The expectation was to bus all night and show up the next day to play. The fierce travel caused some players to want to quit from burn out. The conditions constantly tested the makeup of players. If a home game ended at 10:30 p.m. on a getaway night, for example, players quickly grabbed an unsold hot dog from the concession stands as a postgame meal, hopped on the bus around midnight, and prepared for an all-night bus ride. The travel was like being on a treadmill. They lived on the bus. Fischer explained the brutal travel through Alabama, Florida, Georgia, Tennessee, North Carolina, and South Carolina. "It was extremely difficult and tiring," he said. "We'd arrive in some cities at 9:00 a.m. and have to play that night. We'd rarely play day games on getaway days. It was always a night game and then travel all night. Back then, there wasn't Wi-Fi or TVs on a bus." There weren't any smartphones to help pass time either. A hot commodity for players on the bus was a cassette player to listen to music. Some of them slept, played cards, blasted music, and grabbed the driver's microphone to joke and interview players for an impromptu radio show. They even ragged on the drivers and bonded with them. "Our bus drivers had incredible personalities and we gave them so much shit," Thoma recalled. "They became a part of the team."

Brian Dorsett remembered some fun moments with the drivers when the bus broke down. "Some of our most fun times were on the bus," he said. "One of our drivers was a guy named Weldon Elliott and that was the year Bill Elliott, the speed racer, was dominating NASCAR. Weldon was a small guy with a strong southern accent. I'd get on the microphone in front of the bus and interview him like he was racing as we were going down the road. I was commentating on the race and would break off and interview him. I acted like he was in last place and being passed by everybody. I told him, 'You have to get going,' and we were suddenly flying through the mountains. We had some long bus rides that were fun." Mark Bauer recalled the entertainment when the bus stalled and needed repair. Different sides of players showed up during the downtime. "Rocky Coyle was a comedian," he said. "He used to perform stand-up as we sat on the road." Belcher remembered Polonia and Canseco sprinting on Interstate 40 when the bus stalled. "They were playing chicken with the freeway traffic in the middle of the night," Belcher said.

Keith Lieppman, who managed in the Minors for decades, described the travel that oftentimes forced managers to tap a driver with a fungo bat to keep them awake on the road. "Traveling in the Southern League is tough," he said. "You're always on the bus on fog-ridden roads during early morning hours when managers are trying to keep bus drivers awake. Because teams usually leave right after a ball game, you don't sleep very soundly. So, it can take a toll. From Birmingham to Huntsville, to Orlando, to Jacksonville, there's quite a bit of travel." Conklin remembered a twenty-two-hour ride to Jacksonville. After arriving at 10:00 a.m., Stromer and Conklin decided to visit a beach. They grabbed room keys, beach towels and started walking on a highway. "We're going to the beach after a twenty-two-hour bus ride," Conklin said. "We were young and rambunctious. Fischer saw us when we returned and reminded us of a game that day. He was not going to put up with any of that."

Playing in the California League in 1984, Cadaret said the cities were all within four hours of each other. The teams there usually traveled to a city the morning of a game since they were near each other. Traveling was more complicated and inconvenient for him in 1985, especially since he never has been able to sleep soundly on a bus. The chaos and dysfunction sometimes showed up in his game performances. "After leaving at midnight, we're rolling into Jacksonville, Florida, the next day. Our hotel room was usually not ready because check-in was at 3:00 p.m. I remember sitting on a curb in Jacksonville the day of one of my first starts of the season. It was hot. I was up all night and couldn't get in my room. I was gassed and lasted only three innings that game." Steinbach said the club could have sulked because of the travel and flopped on the field, but they stepped up. "It was about building character," he said.

But at the ballpark, the Stars enjoyed their share of laughs and adventures that came from being a first-place club. "It was a tightknit group on the road, and we didn't have a lot of separate pods," Stromer said. "We did a lot of things together." One prank that brought many players together came from a cage that Joe Mays built. He claimed the cage contained a muskrat and gave it to groundskeeper Crute to frighten players for fun. The concealed cage only exposed the critter's tail. To this day, the kind of animal in the cage is a mystery to many players. To scare new players on the club, and even opposing ones, Crute lured them to his maintenance shack beyond the right-field fence. He warned them not to come close to the cage or the muskrat would attack. But when some players were tempted to look closer, Crute released a spring that popped the muskrat out. It shocked and terrified them. Bauer arrived in May and was a victim right away. "It scared the hell out of me," he said. "You'd walk inside the shed, and he'd pull this thing that made it shoot out. Everyone laughed. It was a team-building sort of thing." Not everyone felt the same chemistry. The late Bob Mayes, a beat writer who had run-ins with some players, said he received backlash for some of his coverage. "Some of them absolutely hated me, but there were some really good guys on the team," Mayes said in 2007.

Away from the drama and on the diamond, Conklin enjoyed hearing Lynyrd Skynyrd's "Sweet Home Alabama" playing at the stadium during the seventh inning stretch. It was an adjustment. He was conditioned to hear "Take Me Out to the Ball Game" that inning. Stars relievers grabbed a bat, pretended to play the guitar, and danced around the bullpen. The song energized the crowd. As a utility player, Conklin wandered to the bullpen on occasions when he wasn't in the lineup. He felt it broke the monotony of always sitting in the dugout. Besides seeing hot girls up close, he bonded with season-ticket holders sitting behind the bullpen. Conklin didn't only network down there, he sometimes got up and warmed up relievers. But as much as Conklin loved helping, he established boundaries: he refused to warm up Cadaret, his roommate in Modesto the previous season. Warming up Cadaret, a flame-throwing lefty, was dangerous. "He threw the ball hard and did not always know where it was going," Conklin chuckled. "I was not going to catch him. When he warmed up, someone else had to come and catch him. I was not willing to take two or three off the shins or the cup." Conklin and Cadaret remain friends today. But camaraderie among teammates didn't mean anything in the standings. Huntsville needed to prove they weren't a fluke when they opened the second half in Birmingham.

11

Boys of Summer

"We were not in Huntsville to stay. Everyone's goal was to get to Triple-A or the big leagues. The locals needed to get accustomed to losing players. They weren't comfortable about it out of the chute. Then they figured how it worked."—**TERRY STEINBACH**, former designated hitter, Huntsville Stars, 2020

Karl Kuehl, Oakland's director of player development, came to Birmingham on June 24, 1985, to catch a doubleheader between the Stars and Barons at Rickwood Field to open the second half. As excited as the Stars were about their first-half success, some wondered how long Oakland would keep the club together, especially given Tacoma's struggles on the West Coast. "Kuehl took a very strong interest in his prospects," Rick Stromer said. "He monitored what they did on and off the field." Back in Huntsville, meanwhile, many fans were growing attached to their favorite players on the team and conditioned to seeing them play. To many fans, the group of players who opened the season in Huntsville represented the community's early connection with the team. They made players feel part of the community. The way the club cast a spell on the city made some fans ignore any other baseball narrative unfolding around the country. The cast of characters on the club was part of a thrill for them that started in April. But considering the fluid nature of the Minor Leagues, constant player movement—including decisions on trading, releasing, promoting, and demoting players—could even dampen a heated pennant race in the Minors or a baseball awakening in a city. Huntsville was not immune to such cruel politics.

Plus, as much as the farmhands were enjoying the celebrity in Huntsville, reaching the Major Leagues was the goal of each player. "We were not in Huntsville to stay," said Terry Steinbach. "Everyone's goal was to get to Triple-A or the big leagues." Even some fans needed reminding that players were not there to stay, and they didn't take losing them too well. A group of fans protested when fan favorite Rocky Coyle was sent to Madison in early June. In May, Charlie O'Brien was promoted to Oakland. The loyal fan base needed to get used to seeing players leave.

A big test came right away to start the second half when Oakland promoted All-Star pitcher Eric Plunk, Huntsville's ace, to Tacoma. Plunk was 8-2 with a 3.67 earned run average for the Stars. He was replacing an injured Jeff Kaiser in Tacoma. "He was dominating," Brad Fischer said of Plunk. "He had a heavy-sinking fastball and a slider. He was a big part of our staff."

Rumors swirled that Jose Canseco, another All-Star and fan favorite—the Southern League's top slugging prospect—would be the next one heading to Tacoma. Some speculated he was being promoted directly to the Majors. He captured Huntsville's heart early when he went on a home run terror during the inaugural home stand. Nicknamed "Parkway Jose" by fans, Canseco drew a cult following there with his tape-measure homers. Despite missing twenty-three games from injury in May, Canseco was Minor League Baseball's top player with twenty homers and sixty-five runs batted in to compliment a .330 batting average. He was on pace to shatter the league's home run record of 42 in a season and Steve Balboni's RBI record of 122 in 1980 when he starred for the Nashville Sounds. The A's scouting report on Canseco was that he had more raw ability than anyone in the organization. Oakland's plan was to keep him in Huntsville the entire season and Kuehl even assured Fischer of that before the doubleheader. "He told me they were leaving Canseco in Huntsville for the rest of the season," Fischer said. "They wanted him to have a big year and move him to Triple-A the next year."

A Southern League doubleheader featured a pair of seven-inning games. Canseco changed Kuehl's mind during the first one. He blasted three homers and drove in nine runs to cap his 5-for-5 hitting parade that included a sixth inning grand slam. Canseco's fireworks led the club's eighteen-hit attack as they crushed the Barons 17–1 in the seven-inning game. His nine RBIS tied Tommie Reynolds's league record set with Birmingham in 1964. Canseco maintained he used a cracked bat for each of his at bats in the game because he ran out of them. A's outfielder Dwayne Murphy gave him the bat in spring training. "We couldn't afford bats back then," Canseco said. "We're not making much in the Minor Leagues and bats were $120 each. Whatever bats I could pick up from a big leaguer during spring training, I did. I put four or five wooden nails in the bat. I cracked it halfway through the game and kept putting nails in it. I can't believe how long it lasted. I was 5 for 5 using a cracked bat." Darrel Akerfelds, meanwhile, earned his seventh win of the season. The Stars lost the second game to the Barons 9–3, but Canseco dominated the headlines and persuaded Kuehl to promote him to Tacoma. "Kuehl told me in between games they reconsidered, and we'd have Canseco for another week because they were moving him to Triple-A," Fischer said. "The game ended with him on deck with the bases loaded. It was one of those games that may never be repeated."

The news of Canseco's departure saddened many fans. He was a superhero to them. This one shook the fan base. Some thought he never wanted to leave. "Fans weren't happy with it," Bob Mayes said in 2007. "He was saying he wanted to stay in Huntsville because he loved it so much. Fans loved him and he loved them. There's no question he was the darling of the fans. They were very unhappy he left." During his three-month stay in Huntsville, Canseco posted freakish numbers: He hit twenty-five homers and drove in eighty runs in only fifty-eight games. He batted .318. Canseco recalled his offensive explosion in Rocket City. "My stats in Huntsville were ridiculous, but the distance of my home runs was even more ridiculous," Canseco said. "I remember opposing coaches saying in the paper they needed to stop me. But I'd hit two more home runs the next day. The whole league tried to stop me. Every pitching staff tried to stop me, but they just couldn't. It was ridiculous." He may have sparked fear in opposing pitchers, but he warmed up to the community. Batboy David Sharp said Canseco was kind to him and never became arrogant from the attention he was receiving. "He took me under his wing and was very nice to me," Sharp said. "He knew where he was headed and didn't get a big head." Canseco's final game in Huntsville that season was on July 1, a Monday night. Don Mincher acknowledged Canseco for his spectacular season in front of the crowd before the game. Fans rushed the Stars' ticket office to secure tickets for Canseco's final game. Fans mobbed him for his autograph before he left. He paid homage to Bob Watson for his improvement. "He helped me a lot with seeing the ball and keeping my shoulders in," Canseco said that day. He joined Tacoma on July 2—his twenty-first birthday.

To replace Canseco on the roster, the club recalled Coyle from Madison. He was hitting .333 with an on-base percentage of .444 for the Muskies in twenty-four games since arriving. The Stars replaced Plunk with a Modesto farmhand. Twenty-four-year-old lefty Pete Kim Kendrick, who was 9-4 with a 2.78 earned run average for the California League club, joined Huntsville on June 30.

With the flashy Canseco era in Huntsville closed by July, the Stars had a season to finish. The club took on a new look without the home run terror. "We suddenly became a team of unsung heroes," Ray Thoma said. Canseco's absence never stalled the team's drive and confidence to win. "We lost him, but it didn't stop us," Brian Dorsett said. After a long drive from Madison, the stocky and gritty Coyle returned to Joe Davis Stadium on July 2 to face Birmingham with a "Welcome Back, Rocky" sign greeting him in the outfield. He was in the starting lineup. Coyle inherited a hard act to follow, but knew he belonged. Taking over in right field for the departed Canseco, Coyle sparked the club right away. He banged two singles in a 5–3 Huntsville win. "Rocky knew the community embraced him," said Dave Tolbert. "He inspired them with his hustle. He played like Pete Rose, always hustling." Coyle said returning to Huntsville after a month in Madison was rewarding and reunited him with his fans, teammates, and family. As hurt and confused as he was for being dropped from one of Minor League Baseball's best teams, he played hard for the Muskies. He had never been demoted in pro baseball before. The move demoralized him. Oakland's best prospects were gathered in Huntsville, and he was suddenly playing in a lower classification. Coming back to Huntsville energized him even more. "I was excited to be back, and the reception was amazing," said Coyle. "People were going nuts when I came to bat. Coming back was a relief on my family because we still had a lease from an apartment we rented there. While I was playing in Madison, my wife had to live with her mother in New Jersey. It was great to be reunited with her in Huntsville and get going again."

The Stars morphed into a speedy, scrappy, and aggressive club once Coyle returned. Fischer explained Coyle's influence on the club on and off the field. His hustle rubbed off on teammates. "Rocky held things together," Fischer said. "He was one of the most important players on the team. Players respected him as a player and person. Everyone gravitated to him." Coyle said despite losing key players to promotions, the remaining players and coaches had already formed a bond with each other. The club was determined to keep gelling and winning. The Stars were now playing without a superstar and the attention that followed one. "We had to just focus and play baseball," Coyle said. "There wasn't any sadness. We had already established a love for each other. They took some key guys, but other ones stepped up. We had to stay consistent and win in front of the fans who came to watch us win."

While Oakland stood clear of Huntsville's prospects in the first half, the second half was a different story. The Stars felt turbulence with roster turnover. Greg Cadaret, who was 3-7 with a 6.12 earned run average, was sent to Modesto in early July. Cadaret was one of the five pitchers in Huntsville's starting rotation to open the season. Two of Modesto's starting pitchers, Rick Rodriguez, a right-hander who was 8-1, and lefty Randy Harvey, 4-2, were promoted to Huntsville. Rodriguez and Harvey joined Kendrick, Mooneyham, and Bauer as other Modesto hurlers joining Huntsville that summer. Coming off an elbow injury, pitcher Tom Dozier, a right-hander, also joined Huntsville in July. Dozier's arrival sparked the rotation. He was 5-2 with a 3.17 earned run average for the Stars in twelve games before being recalled to Tacoma in August. Dozier earned Player of the Week and Month honors in the league during his brief stay in Huntsville. Todd Burns, another right-handed starter, and outfielder Bobby Gould arrived from Madison in August. Only Belcher and Akerfelds were mainstays in the rotation from the group of five starters that opened the season. Mike Ashman, a jack-of-all-trades versatile infielder, joined Huntsville from Tacoma in July. "The biggest challenge I had was contending with all the changes," Fischer said in 1985. "We had fifteen or sixteen changes during the course of the season. We had a revolving door on the clubhouse." Stromer, an infielder, left the club in late July with a season-ending back injury. "I slid in a dugout and ruptured a bunch of vertebrae," Stromer said. "I couldn't finish the season and they sent me home." Shortstop Brian Guinn showed up from Modesto in August.

Fischer's consistent formula in the second half was emphasizing stolen bases and hit and runs to fuel the offense. The top of the lineup, Polonia and Javier, for example, were more active on the bases, instead of relying on a Canseco or Nelson home run. The new scouting report on the Stars was to keep Polonia and Javier off the bases and silence the thump of Dorsett and Nelson. Javier and Polonia swiped a combined total of one hundred bases for Huntsville in 1985. Javier snatched sixty-one and Polonia, thirty-nine. Polonia was mastering a drag bunt down the first-base line and finished the season with eighteen triples, one shy of Alan Trammell's 1977 league record of nineteen, playing for the Montgomery Rebels. Javier, meanwhile, was on the heels of Alvin Davis's league record for most walks in a season. Playing for the Chattanooga Lookouts, Davis drew 120 walks in 1983. Javier finished the season with 112. "I think we've become a more aggressive team on the field," Fischer said in the second half. "There is no way to replace a person like Canseco, so we had to change our way of doing things."

Since the Stars already had clinched a playoff spot, there was little incentive for them to win the second half other than playing for pride and development. They were still a tough team to beat, though.

The club highlighted some of the league's top offensive categories. Nelson and Mark Funderburk of the Orlando Twins battled for home run supremacy during the summer. By September Funderburk had thirty-four and Nelson, thirty-two. Javier was breathing down the neck of Orlando's Alexis Marte for the stolen base lead. More importantly, after a slow first two weeks of the second half, the Stars, 19-13 and an overall record of 58-45, led the Western Division by late July. But a hungry second-place Knoxville club was stalking them. Knoxville, Toronto's Double-A club, played with a chip on their shoulder. After watching Huntsville, a new league entry, take the first half and clinch a playoff berth on their grounds at Bill Meyer Stadium on June 20, they wanted to prove something. They were division champions the previous season and determined to win the second half. Knoxville never let up on the Stars.

As the division race heated up, so did Kendrick, who suddenly emerged as Huntsville's new ace. The club needed Kendrick's rise. Born in Honolulu, Hawaii, on January 4, 1961, Kendrick was a winner, and tough. Growing up, the five-foot-nine, 160-pound lefty dominated on the mound and was a big-game pitcher. He could hit, too. Kendrick, a central Oahu native, led Radford High School to a flawless 20-0 record his senior year in 1979. He declined a free ride to the University of Hawaii and opted for Brigham Young University in Provo, Utah, to pursue a degree in computer science and pitch. Earning the nickname "P.K.," he didn't miss a beat. He was a poised and durable pitcher for the Cougars. On May 18, 1981, Kendrick, a sophomore, remarkably completed both games of a doubleheader against UH to capture the Western Athletic Conference championship. He threw 122 pitches in the first game and 135 in the second one for a total of 257 in sixteen innings that day. He allowed a total of three earned runs for both games. The first game was seven innings. Kendrick quietly had the heart of a bull. He was calm and unemotional on the mound. "If we had to go a third game, I would have told coach to use me in relief," Kendrick said in 1981. Five days later, he pitched another nine-inning complete game against the Texas Longhorns. In 1981 he tossed five shutouts, two no-hitters, and fourteen complete games in nineteen appearances for BYU. He was 29-8 with a 3.08 ERA in his three years at the university. Oakland scout Grady Fuson was interested enough to draft him in the nineteenth round of the June Amateur Draft in 1982. Climbing Oakland's system, the small and durable lefty pitched in relief for Double-A Albany in 1984 but was used primarily as a starter in Modesto in 1985. He wasn't intimidating, towering, and overpowering like Huntsville's other starters, but he earned a lot of favor in his manager's eyes. By mid-July Kendrick was 3-1 since taking over Plunk's spot in the rotation. He featured a slurve, a nasty, sweeping slider, in his arsenal. "He was very dependable and had a great curveball," Fischer said. "He was a low-key, quiet kid."

As the Stars battled through July, off the field, the front office announced a move of their own. Mincher, the general manager, took a medical leave of absence on July 22. He was battling high blood pressure. Mincher had poured his soul into making the Stars a success in Huntsville since September 1984, and the stresses from his duties caught up to him. He was exhausted and needed a break. Kent Pylant took over Mincher's duties while he was gone.

The long season in Double-A was taking a toll on players, too, and tested their makeup constantly. It was a highly competitive level of the Minor Leagues that humbled the most talented. The classification was loaded with prospects. Most players were on an upward trajectory and hungry. Raw talent was polished and refined in Double-A. Teams played each other so much they had a strategy to pitch and defend players. Talent stood out more at this level than any other one. How players performed in Double-A could make or break them. For example, some farmhands succeed in Single-A but struggle when they reach Double-A and never advance. The level filters talent for the parent clubs. In the 1980s, organizations sometimes promoted Double-A players directly to the big leagues, skipping Triple-A, considered the next level. "In most cases, if they did well in Double-A, they could play in the Majors," Walt Jocketty said. Fischer said reaching that level is a confidence booster for many prospects. "Everyone who makes it to Double-A feels like they have arrived," Fischer said. "When they get there, they feel like they have a chance to play in the Major Leagues." Fischer managed in every level and insisted that Double-A was the most fun, exciting, and competitive of all of them. Coyle explained the stiff competition of making the jump from Single-A. "There are limited spots," he said. "Two rosters need to form a small one."

Keith Lieppman managed Tacoma in 1985 and was Oakland's farm director for twenty-eight years. He described the uniqueness of the classification. "Double-A has always been the level that separated players," said Lieppman. "It's far more sophisticated than Single-A. You notice how players adapt and adjust to failure at a much greater level. It weeded out a lot of players. It shows whether a player can handle the difficulties of the sport. Back then, you didn't have many days off, and rain in the Southern League delayed games into the night. The conditions kept pushing and challenging you."

Fischer saw firsthand the humbling nature of playing in Double-A and the pressure players face. He recalled when Javier was scuffling at the plate in the summer. The Stars were trailing the Memphis Chicks at Tim McCarver Stadium in miserable, sweltering conditions, and Javier struck out in his second at bat of the game. Javier returned to the dugout and threw his helmet and bat in disgust before disappearing in a tunnel connected to the clubhouse underneath the bleachers.

Javier had already played in seven games for the New York Yankees in 1984 after being promoted from Double-A Nashville and Triple-A Columbus. He was one of New York's top prospects. The twenty-year-old, smooth-fielding outfielder came to Oakland by virtue of the Rickey Henderson trade in December. He was frustrated about starting the season in Double-A, since he had already played with the Yankees the season before. But even Javier wasn't immune from the sharks of Double-A. When the inning ended, Javier was missing in centerfield for defense. Fischer wondered where he was, and someone told him he was in the clubhouse and not returning. "He was ready to quit," Fischer said. "He told me, 'I can't do this anymore; the pressure is too much.'" Fischer encouraged Javier in the clubhouse, and he eventually trotted back to centerfield. "We talked through it and got him back on the field," Fischer said. "It showed the kind of pressure these kids feel. After that, he started taking off." From the first week of July, Javier raised his average from .240 to .285.

The dog days of August were a rollercoaster and sometimes tumultuous for Huntsville to end the season. They battled with Knoxville for first place the entire month. Fans continued to file inside the new stadium for the club's promotions. The Stars partnered with Burger King to produce a set of team cards. On August 16 the Stars gave the official set of baseball cards to the first three thousand fans arriving to the game. The second half also brought some rare sightings. In a 7–4 loss to Memphis on August 14, Fischer brought Steinbach in to pitch the eighth and Ashman the ninth. They retired the side in order each inning. Newcomers helped the club and the regulars played hard. Newly arriving Todd Burns tossed a 5–0 shutout against Memphis on August 15, and Polonia laid down a successful squeeze bunt in the same game. Polonia had taken a brief excused leave of absence from the club and Coyle took over as leadoff hitter until he returned on August 7.

One of the highlights of the second half was the Stars taking a doubleheader from Charlotte on August 25 at home. In the first game, the Stars came from behind in dramatic fashion. Down 3–1 in the bottom of the ninth, Steinbach drilled a two-run double to tie the game, and Coyle ended it with a game-winning single for a 4–3 win. Thanks to another game-winning hit from Coyle in the second game, the red-hot Stars beat Charlotte 4–1. The doubleheader was Huntsville's final home date of the regular season with exciting news coming forth. The club announced a regular season attendance of 302,796, leading the league. Before the season, Mincher hoped for a season attendance of 250,000. Conway Twitty, part owner of the Stars, electrified the crowd with a postgame concert. Minor League Baseball was a smash hit in Huntsville. "It was a special summer," Mark Mincher said. "There were tremendous crowds that year. We got spoiled with a once-in-a-lifetime team and the newness of pro baseball. We had a team that united us, and we gathered at Joe Davis Stadium." The sweep also widened Huntsville's first-place lead over Knoxville to three and a half games.

After winning the next game in Memphis 4–1, Huntsville, 39-27, was cruising to a second-half championship with seven road games left before the first round of playoffs. In fact, they had a magic number of four at one point. But the Stars needed to play a critical four-game series in Knoxville to end the season. The travel was annoying. The bus broke down on their way to Knoxville and the team was forced to sleep on nearby grass during repairs. It set the tone for a frustrating end of the season. After the club matched their first-half win total of thirty-nine, they never won another game in the second half.

Knoxville swept the Stars to end the season and proved to be a hungrier team. Knoxville clinched the division title on September 1 after beating the Stars 6–1. The clubs were headed in opposite directions. While Huntsville finished the season losing seven straight, Knoxville won their final eight to overtake the Stars. Knoxville, 42-30, was set to play the Stars in the first round of playoffs. But if Huntsville had won the second half, too, they were still slated to play Knoxville in the first round, the team with the best overall record.

Knoxville was still angry over losing the Southern League championship to the Charlotte O's in 1984. They were focused on unfinished business. "But the job isn't done," Kash Beauchamp, a Knoxville outfielder, said after clinching the second half. "This is a pre-celebration. This is the bologna. We want the steak." They didn't celebrate with champagne like the Stars did when they clinched the first half. The Stars finished the second half three and a half games behind Knoxville with a 39-34 record. Huntsville boasted an overall record of 78-66, behind Knoxville's 79-64 and Columbus's 79-65. In the Eastern Division, meanwhile, Charlotte won the second half with a 43-31 record. They were slated to play the division's first-half winner—the Columbus Astros—Houston's Double-A club, in the first round. The winner of that series played the winner of the Western Division series between Huntsville and Knoxville for the championship.

A confident Knoxville carried the momentum heading into the best-of-five series starting at Joe Davis Stadium on September 4. After all, they had beaten the Stars nine of their last ten games against them. The first two games were being played in Huntsville, and the final three in Knoxville, if five games were necessary. Knoxville smelled blood, and the Stars needed their swagger back.

12

Champions

"We wanted desperately to repeat and go back-to-back, but Rocky Coyle, a name that will live in infamy for us, had other ideas. We remember great times and we remember heartbreaks. In my life, Rocky's home run was a heartbreak."—JOHN HART, former manager, Charlotte O's, 2021

When manager Brad Fischer announced Huntsville's touted starting rotation of Tim Belcher, Eric Plunk, Darrel Akerfelds, Greg Cadaret, and Joe Law in April, Pete Kendrick was a part of Modesto's starting rotation. Leaving spring training, he couldn't crack the hot new farm club heading to Huntsville. In fact, his name was even being mentioned in a deal that would have netted Oakland a Minor League shortstop. Instead, Kendrick pitched so well in Modesto, he earned a promotion to Huntsville on June 30 and became the rotation's most consistent hurler. He was 6-4 with a 2.45 ERA to finish the 1985 season.

As the season ended on September 2, and the Stars were coming off a miserable collapse, Fischer turned to Kendrick to open the Western Division series against Knoxville on September 4. Fischer needed a boost. The Stars not only ended the season with seven straight losses, but the heart of the order was slumping. They had lost nine of their last ten games to dangerous Knoxville.

Kendrick faced Knoxville's eleven-game winner Mike Yearout at Joe Davis Stadium in Game One. Before the series, a reporter asked Fischer if Kendrick was Huntsville's new ace. "Yeah, I would have to say so, because of his consistency," Fischer responded. "He gives you a good performance almost every time out. He keeps you in the ballgame. He doesn't walk anybody. He makes the long play, and the defense expects that every time he goes out."

The Stars were playing a focused club and Knoxville's manager John McLaren described their determination. "We came close last year when we made it to the playoff finals, losing to Charlotte," he said before the series. "The desire to win it all has kind of carried over. The guys got a taste of it last year. Now, they want the whole thing."

To keep the team focused, Fischer stressed to players that postseason was a fresh start, the third part of their season. He encouraged them to ignore the gloomy records and embrace the new series. Fischer's wishful thinking couldn't kill the momentum Knoxville felt, though. They were the hotter club down the stretch and owned the Stars. As popular as the Stars were, some doubted they could beat Knoxville. "People counted us out," Rocky Coyle remembered. Fischer revealed the rest of the rotation for the best-of-five series. After Kendrick opened the first game, Fischer was handing the ball to Akerfelds and Todd Burns for the next two, and Belcher, if a fourth game was necessary.

Knoxville haunted Huntsville into the first game of the series. In front of a crowd of 2,832, the Stars came out swinging. Steinbach and Thoma each blasted two-run homers, but Knoxville beat them 9–5 to take a 1–0 lead in the series. Kendrick gave up four earned runs and couldn't escape the fifth. The club committed three errors. The loss disgusted many players. Rob Nelson, who struck out to end the game and committed an error at first, slammed his helmet on the ground and threw his bat. Tempers flared in Huntsville's clubhouse after their eighth consecutive loss. Players barked at Bob Mayes, the Stars' beat writer for the *Huntsville Times*, for bringing up a ball Coyle had fumbled in right field in the fifth inning to allow a run to score. Players were furious. Some of them already had a testy relationship with the reporter. "We came to Rocky's defense and got in Bob's face," Chip Conklin said. "We gave him a hard time. He didn't deserve it, but we were young and passionate. Maybe it was my immaturity." Conklin, though, believed the clubhouse dramatics brought the club closer. It demonstrated the support teammates had for each other. "We were already a tight group and it brought us even tighter," Conklin noted. "It gave us more oomph than we already had and pushed us through." Thoma contended the incident was a "wakeup call that we were going to stick up for each other."

But leaving the clubhouse that Wednesday night, the Stars chances of a championship looked bleak. They faced the fear of being a bust. Losing to Knoxville at home was discouraging and Huntsville didn't start the second game any better. Knoxville's Chris Johnston blasted a grand slam off Akerfelds in the first to take a quick 4–0 lead. The Stars trailed Knoxville 8–3 in the seventh and were nine outs away from being down 0–2 heading to the road. But they came out of nowhere to roar back with eleven runs over the next two innings to fuel a 14–10 win over Knoxville to tie the series at 1–1. In front of 2,295 fans, Nelson took care of business. He was 2 for 3 with a homer and scored three runs. Knoxville, this time, committed five errors. Reliever Randy Harvey got the win for Huntsville, and Scott Whaley, the save. The remarkable Game Two comeback eased the club's mounting burden. The shocking loss buckled Knoxville's knees. "This gets a huge burden off my shoulders and the shoulders of my players," Fischer said after the game. "We've been carrying this thing around with us. It's been in the back of our minds for a long time. Finally, the momentum has shifted. It's on our side."

Although Huntsville's win was only their first since August 26, Fischer was right. The comeback win brought momentum to the Stars, and Knoxville never recovered. In Game Three, Burns, Harvey, and Whaley allowed Knoxville only four hits to lead the Stars to a 5–2, twelve-inning win at Bill Meyer Stadium. Steinbach, the designated hitter, hit the go-ahead home run in the twelfth inning to knock down Knoxville with 1,257 fans on hand. Knoxville was suddenly facing elimination with Belcher pitching for the Stars in the fourth game. "Our backs are to the wall," McLaren said after the devastating loss. Belcher, Javier, and Polonia knocked Knoxville from the postseason in Game Four. The sparkplugs, Polonia and Javier, drove in a combined seven runs, and Belcher tossed a masterful three-hit, 7–0 shutout. He struck out eight batters. "It was Tim's best performance of the year," Fischer said. It couldn't have come at a better time for the Stars, who were advancing to the championship series. Polonia was 3 for 5 with four RBIS to fuel Huntsville's fourteen-hit attack. Steinbach had a monster series at the plate. He was 9 for 20, with two homers and seven RBIS in the four games. The club was now riding the momentum of a three-game winning streak. Coyle reflected on beating Knoxville in the first round. "We lost all those games at the end of the season, and everyone said we choked," he said. "We ended up beating a really good Knoxville club with a lot of future big leaguers. They wrote us off."

On the same night the Stars were advancing, the Charlotte O's clinched the Eastern Division series in four games with a 7–3 win over Columbus. The Stars and O's were facing off in the championship series that started on September 9. Like the Knoxville series, the first two games were being played in Huntsville and the next three in Charlotte, if necessary. Playing at Joe Davis Stadium was a house of horrors for Charlotte all season. The O's had won only one of eight games there. The Stars did not fare any better at Crockett Park, Charlotte's ballpark, where they had lost six of eight games. Charlotte, the defending league champions, presented a greater challenge to the Stars. While Knoxville had future Major League talent, the O's fielded some former big leaguers. They batted .292 in the Columbus series. The O's were playing for their third championship in six years. John Hart, Charlotte's thirty-seven-year-old manager, had taken over for Grady Little in June 1984. The O's were in last place with a record of 29-43. Hart turned the club around and led them to a championship that season. He wanted another one in 1985. "We wanted desperately to repeat and go back-to-back," remembered Hart.

Charlotte was only three wins away from another championship, but there were challenges early for the franchise. Three weeks before the season, on March 16, a fire destroyed forty-four-year-old Crockett Park during spring training. The front office needed to come up with a plan to make the facility suitable for baseball by April. They placed a temporary stadium, including portable bleachers, on top of the ruins. Mark Wiley, another manager in Baltimore's organization, broke the news to Hart. "I thought he was kidding," Hart said. "They put in little portable grandstands, and we had to shower in trailers. It was unbelievable. We played the entire season in sort of a makeshift situation." The stadium still lacked a grandstand roof because of the fire. Despite the inconveniences, the O's were hungry. Winning another championship under the circumstances would be heartwarming for the franchise and community.

Fischer turned to Kendrick again to open the best-of-five series, and Hart tapped eleven-game winner Tony Arnold. Kendrick had a rocky start to open the division series, but Fischer wanted him on the mound against Charlotte. So did his teammates. Coyle, while playing for the University of Arizona a few years earlier, played against Kendrick and noticed his toughness. He also played summer ball with Kendrick in Alaska. "Of all the great pitchers I played with, if I needed a win, I wanted Kendrick to throw the clutch game," Coyle said. "He was tough and should have played in the big leagues. I felt confident when he was on the mound. We didn't miss a beat with him."

Akerfelds and Burns were scheduled to follow Kendrick, with Belcher looming for Game Four, if necessary. Hart's strategy was to control Huntsville's running game and keep the pesty Polonia and Javier off the bases. The Stars were confident. "Charlotte was a good club, but we were better," said closer Wayne Giddings. The Stars faced the pressure of not bringing Huntsville a championship with such a star-studded club. Kendrick took control of the first game, and Huntsville's offense gifted him with more than enough run support. The Stars thumped the O's 11–1 in front of 2,876 at Joe Davis Stadium to take a 1–0 series lead. The club was two wins away from a championship. A poised Kendrick, who baffled batters with his tantalizing slurve, went the distance and allowed only one run and four hits. "Pete was solid and always had guts," Brian Dorsett said. "He wanted to prove he was a prospect. That was his mentality. He was a big plus for us down the stretch. It was neat he had that kind of success." Brian Guinn hit a two-run homer in the seventh, and Javier was 3 for 5 and drove in two runs to fuel the offense. Fischer said after the game that Javier was the best example of Huntsville's style of play in the second half. "Occasional power, speed, stealing bases, putting the ball on the plate with good defense, is why I picked Javier," Fischer said. The win was the club's fourth consecutive of the playoffs.

The big news before Game Two was that Akerfelds was not taking the mound as expected. He was battling shoulder soreness that plagued him all season. Mark Bauer replaced him. Being used primarily as a starter, Bauer was 5-8 with a 4.74 earned run average for the Stars. He opened the season in Modesto and was promoted directly to Tacoma before being sent down to Huntsville in May. "Going from Single-A to Triple-A was a lot," Bauer recalled. "I came to Huntsville after those guys had already been there a month." He had already pitched for Double-A Albany the previous season and even boasted strong numbers. He was 7-2 with a 2.30 earned run average. Because of the fierce competition to make the Huntsville club, he started the season in Modesto. "I was pitching the best I ever had in Albany, so I was disappointed to start the season in Single-A," he said. Bauer was pitching for a championship in 1985.

Bauer's mound counterpart was All-Star right-hander John Habyan, who was 13-5 for Charlotte. Game Two was the final game of the season at Joe Davis Stadium and workers were preparing the multipurpose facility for high school football. As 3,253 fans watched, Bauer tossed eight strong innings and Dorsett spanked an 0-2 pitch for a two-out, game-winning single in the bottom of the ninth to secure Huntsville's 4–3 win. Thoma provided the defensive play of the game. With the O's rallying in the fourth, Steve Padia drilled a ball that Thoma speared at third. Thoma then tagged the base to double off the runner and kill the rally. Fans gave the Stars a standing ovation before leaving the field and heading to Charlotte for Game Three. The loss was Charlotte's ninth in ten games in Huntsville for the season. The O's were happy to leave Huntsville. "I'm sick of this ballpark," Hart said after the game. "We just don't play well here. I'm glad to get out of here." The Stars led the series 2–0 and were one win away from a championship.

If the Stars won the championship, they would have to celebrate in Charlotte and not in front of the home crowd. The remaining games were being played at Crockett Park. "It was a bummer we had to play on the road for the championship," Dorsett said.

The Stars were playing in a portable stadium in Charlotte, but they were serious about winning Game Three. "It was a glorified high school park but had a playoff feel," Bauer said. "Charlotte was a good team." Coyle felt the postseason vibes on the Wednesday night. "The excitement in Charlotte was insane," he said. "They were battlers and so were we." Charlotte cooled Huntsville down in the third game in front of 1,930 fans. Burns, making his second start of the postseason, coughed up homers to Kelvin Torve and Tommy Dodd in the fifth as Charlotte edged the Stars 3-2 to halt any celebration. Dorsett clubbed a two-run dinger in the eighth for Huntsville's only runs. There was more bad news for the Stars. Coyle tore his left hamstring sliding into second base in the game. The tear was so severe, the club determined he was done for the season. The Stars now led the series 2-1 with Belcher on the mound for Game Four.

The limping Coyle was not in Huntsville's lineup for Game Four, and the versatile Ashman replaced him in right. Coming into the game, the Stars wanted desperately to avoid playing a decisive Game Five at Crockett Park, where they were 2-7. The Stars were confident with Belcher on the mound. He was dominant in Huntsville's series-clinching Game Four win over Knoxville. Belcher eliminated Knoxville and wanted to do the same to Charlotte. It looked ugly early for the O's. The Stars, facing former big leaguer Rick Steirer, erupted for nine runs in the second inning, highlighted by a Nelson grand slam, to take a 9-0 lead over Charlotte after only two innings. Belcher was dealing early. He fanned six of the first seven batters. Everyone figured the resilient Stars were on their way to a championship that night. But Charlotte chipped away at the lead and battled back with two runs in the third and three in the fourth to make the game 9-5. The Stars were up 10-8 in the eighth when Charlotte's Terry Bogener clubbed a two-run bomb and Jeff Kenaga raked a solo shot to highlight a dramatic and improbable come-from-behind 11–10 win for the O's. Huntsville was shocked, and Charlotte carried the momentum from the dramatic win into the championship game. The O's and Stars were tied 2–2 in the series. "The series was a battle all the way through," Hart said. For the dejected Stars, coming off a traumatizing loss and blowing a 2–0 series lead, playing Game Five in Charlotte was daunting. Some doubted they could win. But Thoma said the club never doubted. "We never thought we blew our chance, or the season was over," he said. "No one gave up."

Kendrick, the laid-back lefty, got the nod for the decisive, final game of the season on September 13, and Hart countered with Arnold. Kendrick was the winning pitcher in Game One of the series. Since pitching for Radford High in the late 1970s, he was conditioned to pitch in big games. Coyle, meanwhile, limping from his torn hamstring, knew he wasn't in the lineup for Game Five. He called Fischer in the middle of the night and persuaded him to let him play. "I told him to put me in the game," Coyle said. "He put me low in the order. I had to fight to get in the lineup." Coyle batted eighth.

Three thousand fans filled Crockett Park for Game Five. Huntsville struck early off Arnold with two runs in the first on a Nelson run-scoring single and a John Marquardt groundout. The score remained 2–0 until Charlotte's Jeff Jacobson drilled a two-run triple to tie the score in the fifth. Tommy Dodd's single scored another run for the O's that inning and Charlotte took a 3–2 lead into the eighth. But Ashman, a pinch hitter, countered with a run-scoring double to tie the score at 3 heading into the ninth with Kendrick cruising. Coyle, who was 2 for 3 in the game, led off the top of the ninth. "I was hitting the ball well," Coyle said. Right-hander Mark Leiter was Charlotte's reliever in the ninth. Leiter was lights out. He tossed two and two-thirds perfect innings of relief the night before in Charlotte's miraculous win. "I remember making the pitching change," Hart said. "He had a good slider." Coyle hobbled to the plate with a hamstring tear and Huntsville's hopes on his shoulders. He saw one of Leiter's sliders and drilled a home run to centerfield to give the Stars a 4–3 lead. "He threw Rocky a hanging slider, and he hit it deep into the night," Hart said. "It broke my heart." Coyle remembered the adrenaline rush and the pain as he trotted around the bases. "I hit the home run with a hole in my hamstring," he said.

Javier added another run in the inning with a single to push the Stars lead to 5–3 heading to the bottom of the ninth. After Kendrick retired the first two batters, he got catcher Carl Nichols to fly out to right fielder Bobby Gould for the final out and championship. Kendrick retired the side in order and fired a complete game five-hitter in the Stars' 5–3 win. He was 2-0 in the championship series with two complete games. Teammates mobbed him on the field and soaked each other with champagne in the bullpen. "Stars win, Stars win, Stars win!" Rick Davis, the club's radio voice, shouted on air. "The league championship belongs to Huntsville."

In June, Kendrick was pitching in Modesto and Coyle was in Madison. "The Oakland A's told Coyle in midseason he was not a prospect and couldn't play Major League Baseball. . . . They sent him to Madison, and he sat there for a month, and came back here and wins the league championship for us," Davis said on Huntsville's WFIX-AM 1450 broadcast. "How can the guy not be a prospect?" Coyle's home run still haunts Hart. He was 7 for 16 in the series. "We remember great times and we remember heartbreaks," he said. "In my life, Rocky's home run was a heartbreak."

Coyle said winning the championship was even more meaningful to him given he was demoted to Single-A in June. Dave Tolbert compared the heroics of Coyle to underdog Daniel "Rudy" Ruettiger in the 1993 sports film *Rudy*. "He was our 'Rudy' from Notre Dame," Tolbert said. Coyle was a hero in Huntsville and never reached the Majors. After the series, back in Modesto, Greg Cadaret heard about Coyle's spark in the postseason. "The buzz was that he was larger-than-life there," Cadaret said. Larry Schmittou recalled Coyle's heroics. "He was the unsung hero on that team," he said.

Hart tipped his hat to Kendrick. "To me, he was the difference," Hart said after the series. "He's beaten us three times in the last three weeks." Kendrick spoke with Davis on the radio after the game. "I was very nervous inside but didn't want them to see it," Kendrick said. "We came from behind . . . last night's game was a tough one to take, but we came back today and fought like champions and here we are." Kendrick saluted Huntsville on the air. "This is for Huntsville," he said. "Thanks, Huntsville, I enjoyed playing here."

Fischer was elated about beating a tough Charlotte club for the championship. He celebrated his second championship in six years managing in Oakland's system. He led Medford to a Northwest League championship in 1981 at age twenty-five. "They were always a good team, and it was really exciting for us to win, especially being the first year in Huntsville," Fischer said. "We lost key players, but we continued to play okay." Huntsville's winning record in 1985 marked Fischer's fifth consecutive winning season as a manager. Thoma was relieved the powerhouse of a club won a championship the first season. "We had the best team anyone could imagine," Thoma said. "It would have been a shame to blow it." Mark Mincher said winning the championship was icing on the cake for a great season, especially with his father, Don, at the forefront. "To see him take baseball to that level in Huntsville made you proud," Mark said.

Fans celebrated the championship back in Huntsville. To this day, many fans remember listening to the game on the radio when the Stars captured the league title. "One guy told me he was listening to the championship game on a hammock at home with his dad when I hit the home run," Coyle said. "They both fell and started jumping around the backyard. They didn't want it to end." The Stars were presented with the pennant during a championship ceremony at City Hall the following week. Don Mincher and Mayor Joe Davis were on hand.

The championship was a storybook ending to a dream season that united a city and a baseball club. The club's success belonged to the community, too. "The championship meant success for everyone," said David Sharp. "It was a sense of pride. The fans felt a part of it." Joe Davis worked tirelessly to bring the club, and his persistence had paid off in the first season. The Huntsville Stars were champions. "I knew they would be successful, and they exceeded my expectations of how successful," said Schmittou. "The team was full of stars. You could tell right off the bat the team was loaded." Schmittou's new Triple-A Nashville Sounds finished two and a half games behind the Louisville Redbirds in the American Association's Eastern Division in 1985. The Nashville franchise failed to reach the playoffs for the first time since 1978.

The story of the Stars was buzzing around the Minor Leagues. If the first year was any indication, Huntsville was positioned to be one of Minor League Baseball's top brands and franchises. Joe Davis Stadium, state of the art in 1985, set the standard for new Minor League parks. Farmhands geared up to play in Huntsville. The first season proved the city would support a team. The Stars led the league in attendance, convincingly, in a season filled with rain delays. The franchise created an opening act that was hard to follow on all fronts. "We did it all that first season," said Cynthia Giles. "I remember hearing Kent Pylant say that the bad part was there was only one way to go after this season. I didn't want to hear that, but it was true." Huntsville savored the moment and enjoyed the ride while they could.

Epilogue

"For Huntsville baseball fans, it has been a dream season on all fronts. If anything, local fans may eventually find themselves spoiled by the 1985 season. We could have many more seasons and teams and not have one that could match this one."—**BILL MCCUTCHEN**, sports editor, *Huntsville News,* September 1985

The Huntsville Stars, besides winning the championship in 1985, led the Southern League in attendance in their first season of existence. Before the season, general manager Don Mincher hoped to draw 250,000. Over three hundred thousand came through the turnstiles in Huntsville that season. The Stars did not win another championship until 1994, under manager Gary Jones. Joe Davis Stadium became one of Minor League Baseball's top attractions and was dubbed the "Crown Jewel of the Southern League" and "The Joe." The city hosted the Southern League All-Star Game in 1986. In late 1993 Mincher and some local investors purchased the franchise from Larry Schmittou to keep the club in Huntsville. Schmittou, who delivered the franchise to Huntsville in 1984, wanted to focus on his other operation—the Triple-A Nashville Sounds. Schmittou remains a prominent and revered baseball figure in Nashville.

Huntsville hosted Oakland's Double-A farmhands until 1998 when the A's moved them to Midland, Texas. The Milwaukee Brewers brought Huntsville a Double-A team in 1999 and stayed for sixteen seasons. But the newness of Joe Davis Stadium was wearing off, and newer ballparks around the Minors were raising the bar. The neglected stadium was decaying, and fan interest was waning. After an ownership change, the franchise relocated to Biloxi, Mississippi, after the 2014 season and was named the Biloxi Shuckers. The Stars played in Huntsville for thirty seasons. From 1985 to 2014, they compiled a record of 2,112-2,099 with fourteen playoff appearances, including three Southern League championships (1985, 1994, 2001).

Brad Fischer finished second in Southern League Manager of the Year voting in 1985, behind co-winners Carlos Alfonso and John McLaren. By 1986 *Baseball America* crowned him Minor League Manager of the Year. After spending seventeen years in the organization, Fischer finally joined Oakland's staff as a bullpen coach in 1996, thanks to Oakland's new manager, Art Howe. He never reached his dream of managing in the Major Leagues. His managerial record in the Minors was 761-726. Fischer is a Minor League coach with the Pittsburgh Pirates. Pitching coach Gary Lance joined the San Diego Padres organization. Karl Kuehl, Oakland's director of player development for eight years, was promoted to special assistant for baseball operations in 1992. Keith Lieppman took over for Kuehl to oversee player development.

After the season, Jose Canseco was voted the league's Most Valuable Player after playing in only fifty-eight games. He clubbed twenty-five homers and drove in eighty runs with a .318 batting average. He made his Major League debut with Oakland on September 2. In a season for the ages, in three levels of play, he amassed 41 homers with 140 RBIS in 147 games. *Baseball America* crowned him Minor League Player of the Year in 1985. He won the American League Rookie of the Year in 1986 and Most Valuable Player in 1988. He was the first player ever to swipe forty bases and hit forty homers in a season. He later admitted to using performance enhancing drugs in his tell-all book, *Juiced*, released in 2005.

On the mound, Tim Belcher led the Stars with eleven wins, and reliever Wayne Giddings led with twelve saves. Rob Nelson clubbed thirty-two home runs, and Polonia finished the season with eighteen triples, one shy of the league record. Reliever Scott Whaley was a dependable lefty all season. He was 9-4 with a 2.61 earned run average combined at Single-A Madison and Huntsville. Pete Kendrick, even with his postseason heroics, never reached the Majors. Oakland traded Kendrick, Charlie O'Brien, and Steve Kiefer to the Brewers for pitcher Moose Haas before the 1986 season. Some of them were lucky enough to experience the big leagues. Some played longer than others.

By 1987 Canseco, Nelson, Steinbach, Javier, Polonia, Burns, Plunk, and Cadaret were on the Oakland A's roster, and most of them played a part in their resurgence in the late 1980s. As forecasted, they pushed Oakland to three consecutive World Series appearances from 1988 to 1990, including a championship in 1989. Some former Stars went elsewhere. Pitcher Darrel Akerfelds and catcher Brian Dorsett were traded to the Cleveland Indians for second baseman Tony Bernazard in 1987. Nelson, Oakland's starting first baseman at the beginning of the 1987 season, was traded to the Padres for Storm Davis in September. Oakland also traded Belcher to the Los Angeles Dodgers for reliever Rick Honeycutt that year. Belcher was on the mound to start Game 1 of the 1988 World Series against the A's at Dodger Stadium. He coughed up a grand slam to Canseco in the second inning and recorded a win in Game 4 of the series as Los Angeles finished Oakland off in five games to win the championship. Steinbach, a third baseman turned catcher in Huntsville, won the 1988 All-Star Game MVP. In 1989 the A's traded Plunk, Cadaret, and Polonia to the New York Yankees for Rickey Henderson. It marked the second time Plunk was a part of a trade for Henderson. In total, fifteen of the 1985 Stars played in the big leagues: Polonia, Nelson, Javier, Canseco, Plunk, Dorsett, O'Brien, Steinbach, Akerfelds, Burns, Belcher, Cadaret, Tom Dozier, Bill Mooneyham, and Rick Rodriguez. Some of them have found success in real estate and business and some have stayed connected to the game they love—baseball.

To honor Rocky Coyle's leadership, heart, and hustle, the Stars Booster Club created "The Rocky" award in 1992 for the player who "best exemplifies the hustle, team spirit, and love of the game as demonstrated by Rocky Coyle." In 2008, to honor Mincher, the Stars retired the No. 5 jersey, the number he wore most of his playing career. The words "Player," "GM," "Owner," and "Mentor" headlined the banner honoring him next to the right-field foul pole. Mincher and Schmittou were inducted into the Southern League Hall of Fame. Mincher passed on March 4, 2012. He was seventy-three. Mayor Joe Davis, meanwhile, finished his fifth consecutive term in 1988. He died on November 14, 1992, at age seventy-four.

The Huntsville area was without a club for five years until the Rocket City Trash Pandas, a farm club of the Los Angeles Angels, arrived in nearby Madison, Alabama, in 2020. Toyota Field, built in 2018, is the area's new home for professional baseball. Huntsville, boasting a population of more than 215,000, was recognized as Alabama's largest city in a 2020 census, surpassing Birmingham. In May 2022 Huntsville was named the "best place to live in the United States" by U.S. News & World Report's annual ranking. Huntsville officials approved $28 million worth of renovations for what was left of Joe Davis Stadium and transformed it into a modern, year-round, multisport facility. Oakland's Double-A affiliate is still located in Midland.

In Memory

Darrel Akerfelds

Jimmy Bragan

Joe W. Davis

Harvey Dorfman

John Glenn

Pedro Gomez

Walter A. Haas Jr.

Karl Kuehl

Jane W. Mabry

Billy Martin

Eddie Mathews

Bob Mayes

Joe Mays

Don Mincher

H. E. "Hub" Myhand

Ron Plaza

Bill Rigney

George Steinbrenner

Billy Tallent

Jim Talley

Glenn Wallace

Bob Watson

Pete Whisenant

Dick Wiencek

Tom Zmudosky

Acknowledgments

Publicly thanking my Heavenly Father after writing a new book never gets old for me. Thank you, Lord, for giving me the opportunity, grace, courage, focus, and drive to capture the story.

The baseball awakening that took place in Huntsville, Alabama, in 1985 first pulled me while writing my first book, *Bash Brothers*, in 2004. The Stars were Huntsville's first professional baseball club in fifty-five years. They united the city, shattered attendance records in a new stadium, and capped the magical season off with a Southern League championship. The excitement and thrill the Stars brought to Huntsville still resonate with the community today. The club filled a void in the city.

I finally wrote the book proposal in 2020 and found a publishing home. Special thanks to the University of Nebraska Press and Rob Taylor, senior acquisitions editor, for sharing the same enthusiasm for the project. Thank you, Rob, for being an ambassador for so many great baseball books and authors through the years. Thanks to Courtney Ochsner, associate acquisitions editor; Rosemary Sekora, publicity manager; and Leif Milliken, rights and permissions coordinator, for your behind-the-scenes contributions to shepherd the book into existence.

Much appreciation to the incredible media in Huntsville and Nashville who lived through the story and generously shared their time with me to resurrect it: John Pruett, Mark McCarter, Skip Nipper, and the late Bob Mayes. Big thanks to Rick Davis, former radio voice of the

Stars, who was a valuable resource from the jump and connected me with key figures in Huntsville.

Thanks to David Lilly and Heather Adkins of the Huntsville-Madison County Public Library for your hospitality during my stay in Huntsville and follow-up research assistance; to Carol Atchley and Kelly Schrimsher of the city of Huntsville for connecting me with Mayor Tommy Battle; to Huntsville mayor Battle for sharing your memories of 1985.

Finding photos of the story was challenging. Thanks to Meredith McDonough of the Alabama Department of Archives and History for helping me secure wonderful photos for the book to capture the excitement and energy of that season. To photographer Dave Dieter, thanks for capturing many of them.

Interviewing is just one of the many jobs of an author. Special thanks to the many media directors around professional baseball who responded to my requests and connected me with people: Curtis Danburg, Bart Swain, Rob Butcher, Adam Chodzko, Matt Birch, June Napoli, Dustin Morse, John Kocsis Jr., Mark Ling, Catherine Aker, Detra Paige, Kaladon Stewart, and Lindsey Knupp.

Many thanks to Sandy Alderson, Larry Schmittou, Walt Jocketty, Brad Fischer, and John Hart for your generous time and insight to shape the book. To the Mincher family, Patsy, Mark, Donna, and Lori, it was such an honor to learn and write about the late Don Mincher, who lived and breathed Huntsville baseball.

Special thanks to these individuals: Robert Tafoya, Richard Rodriguez, Dave Newhouse, Carl Steward, Josephine Tafoya-Peraza, Bud Geracie, Andy Dolich, Terry Steinbach, Art Spander, Steven Lavoie, Dave Wilder, Dennis Rogers, Stan Javier, Roy Eisenhardt, Ben Bernard, Greg Cadaret, Chip Conklin, Steven Travers, Keith Lieppman, Rocky Coyle, Ray Thoma, Tim Belcher, Wayne Giddings, Rick Stromer, Cynthia Giles, Brian Dorsett, Mark Bauer, Steve Kiefer, Grady Fuson, Sara Springsteen, Jose Canseco, Adam Rifenberick, Carmel Zmudosky, Dave Tolbert, Damon Tolbert, Nancy Finley, John Hickey, Bill McCutchen, Melissa Lockard, David Feldman, Bill Chastain, Mark Heineke, Bridget Barry, Morgan Strelow, Ken Korach, Mark Gonzales, Howard Bryant, Sarah

Valenzuela, Alex Coffey, Shayna Rubin, Carlos Lopez, Nicole Lopez, Joycelyn Lopez, Julie Marques, Glenn Schwarz, Rick Rodriguez, Ken Davidoff, Tyler Kepner, Donald Young, Billy Beane, Mark Bechtel, Dave Stewart, Brian Guinn, Donald Moore, Joe Stiglich, Marquetta Padilla, Alex Padilla Jr., Larry Krueger, Mike Ashman, Mickey Morabito, Mark Ibanez, Charlie O'Brien, Wayne Garland, Bryan Hoch, Tyler Bleszinski, Alex Hall, Christina Kahrl, Bruce Markusen, Shane Thomas-Williams, Bruce Jenkins, Josh Suchon, Lori Webb, David Sharp, Rick Tittle, Ron Barr, Marty Lurie, Joe Salvatore, Paul Gutierrez, Frank Mallicoat, Gabriel Zamora, Amy Andrieux, Steve Kettmann.

My sincere appreciation to the library staffs of the *Huntsville Times*, the *Huntsville News*, the *Boston Globe*, *Athletics Nation*, the *San Francisco Examiner*, the *Oakland Tribune*, the *San Francisco Chronicle*, the *Charlotte Observer*, the *Orlando Sentinel*, the *Modesto Bee*, *Sports Illustrated*, *The Tennessean*, the *Kingsport Times*, the *Commercial Appeal*, the *Atlanta Constitution*, the *Daily Herald*, the *Capital Times*, the *Wisconsin State Journal*, *Baseball America*, the *Sporting News*, the *Bennington Banner*, the *Fresno Bee*, the *Hartford Courant*, the *Post-Star*, the *Evening Sun*, the *Jackson Sun*, the *Marion Star*, the *News-Journal*, the *Indiana Gazette*, the *Tacoma News Tribune*, the *Honolulu Star-Bulletin*, the *Greenville News*, the *Knoxville News-Sentinel*, the *Arizona Daily Star*, the *Arizona Republic*, the *Birmingham Post-Herald*, the *Montgomery Advertiser*, the *Birmingham News*, the *Anniston Star*, the *Alabama Journal*, the *Christian Science Monitor*, the *Cincinnati Enquirer*, the *Great Falls Tribune*, the *Star Tribune*, the *New York Post*, and the *Star-Gazette*. BaseballReference.com, Retrosheet.org, TheBaseballCube.com, and StatsCrew.com were tremendous online resources.

The team was just one part of what made the season special. Fans poured inside Joe Davis Stadium and energized the club. The community did the same for me. Special thanks to the dignitaries, media, and residents of Huntsville for your support.

Notes on Research and Sources

The return of professional baseball in Huntsville almost never happened. In late 1984 city officials initially shot down Larry Schmittou's demand to sell beer in the proposed stadium. He was adamant. If beer sales weren't allowed in the new venue, he wouldn't deliver the franchise to Huntsville. But a compromise between Schmittou and the city council was reached. They agreed on a designated section for nondrinkers, and the city built Schmittou a new stadium for his Double-A franchise. As it turned out, there was little interest in the alcohol-free section. But there was a great deal of interest in seeing the Huntsville Stars play at Joe W. Davis Stadium. The Stars were born when Huntsville craved entertainment and an outlet to bring the community together. The community found a place to gather after work and school. Huntsville embraced the freshness of a new baseball team, and the players rewarded them with a Southern League championship.

Thirty-eight years later, the memories of the baseball revival in Huntsville in 1985 still energize everyone who experienced it—players, executives, fans, scouts, workers, writers, dignitaries, coaches, and businessmen. The city fell in love with the Stars. No one could have predicted the excitement. Oakland's top prospects playing in Huntsville for the inaugural season hypnotized fans. It was a thrill for me to dive into the story.

As magical as the season was, there wasn't a great deal of material available to compile enough detail for a book. I needed to find the principals who lived the story and travel to Huntsville for research in August

2021. Former players Ray Thoma, Rocky Coyle, and Chip Conklin were very generous with their time and stories from the beginning. Huntsville insiders such as Rick Davis and John Pruett shared the same enthusiasm when I interviewed them. Before the late Bob Mayes, the Stars' first beat reporter, passed away in 2016, he offered me great insight into the politics and challenges of covering the team. Brad Fischer, the club's first manager, offered me detail on each of his players. I was delighted to learn that he was one of Minor League Baseball's winningest managers in the 1980s and started managing at age twenty-three. It made sense for Oakland to send him to manage the Huntsville club.

Another part of what made the story special was that the city treated the Minor Leaguers like royalty. The players enjoyed the town and were recognized in supermarkets and restaurants. They were conditioned to play in front of small crowds during their rise through the Minors. A crowd of over ten thousand greeted them in Huntsville for the home opener on April 19, 1985. The players were excited to share their memories of the season. After all, they were there, behind the scenes, at home, in the dugout, in the clubhouse, in hotel rooms, and on long bus rides through the South. Cynthia Giles, the club's former ticket manager, shared her memories of the magical season. Huntsville is recognized for rocketry and space. It was enlightening to learn how the city welcomed a new Minor League team. Huntsville suddenly became known as a baseball hub, and every Minor Leaguer wanted to play at the city's new stadium.

The year 1985 was a memorable one for me. As a freshman in high school, I was an avid baseball card collector and plastered posters of players on my walls. I also enjoyed the classic music and movies of that year. Watching baseball and professional wrestling was a habit for me every Saturday of 1985. My obsession with that year fueled me to capture professional baseball's return to Rocket City, a romance between a team and city. Each player I interviewed emphasized how much the city embraced and celebrated them. Fans grew attached to each player. The politics of the Minor Leagues—including demotions and promotions—was sometimes difficult for them to accept. They wanted the players to stay in Huntsville and keep the excitement going.

In my research, I learned a great deal about life in the Minor Leagues, specifically the Southern League: the travel, host families, the sacrifice, and the Double-A level of pro ball. Keith Lieppman shared stories with me and broke down the life of a Minor Leaguer in 1985.

Interviewing Sandy Alderson, Larry Schmittou, John Hart, and Walt Jocketty was a delight. Each of them played prominent roles in the story. They shared with me intimate details of the circumstances that brought the farm club to Huntsville for the 1985 season. These men are giants in baseball circles today. The Mincher family—Mark and Patsy—gave me great stories and insight into the late Don Mincher, who worked tirelessly to make the Stars a success that season.

Joe Davis, Huntsville's mayor at the time, recognized the charm of what a new team would bring to the community and pushed hard in the face of doubters to land the franchise. Without Davis's persistence there would not have been a new franchise in Huntsville that year. I was excited to interview people who knew Davis and what made him tick.

I spoke with former players, farm directors, dignitaries, front office staff, executives, coaches, broadcasters, managers, clubhouse insiders, historians, authors, owners, fans, and beat writers. Enhancing the interviews, digitized newspaper archives helped me confirm dates and times.

The following is a list of people interviewed once or multiple times for the book: Tim Belcher, Rocky Coyle, John Hart, Stan Javier, Mike Ashman, Sandy Alderson, Walt Jocketty, Ray Thoma, Chip Conklin, Larry Schmittou, Rick Davis, Brad Fischer, Grady Fuson, Jose Canseco, Terry Steinbach, Rick Rodriguez, Mark Bechtel, Mark Bauer, Wayne Giddings, Greg Cadaret, Brian Guinn, John Pruett, Keith Lieppman, Mark McCarter, David Sharp, Rick Stromer, Charlie O'Brien, David Wilder, Brian Dorsett, Mark Mincher, Patsy Mincher, Wayne Garland, Tommy Battle, Skip Nipper, Cynthia Giles, Steven Travers, Ben Bernard, Donald Moore, Carmel Zmudosky, Damon Tolbert, Dave Tolbert, Steve Kiefer, Clifford Pate, and Ernest Kaufmann.

Bibliography

Canseco, Jose. *Juiced: Wild Times, Rampant 'Roids, Smash Hits, and How Baseball Got Big*. New York: Harper Collins, 2005.

Colton, Larry. *Southern League: A True Story of Baseball, Civil Rights, and the Deep South's Most Compelling Pennant Race*. New York: Grand Central Publishing, 2013.

Coste, Chris. *The 33-Year-Old Rookie: My 13-Year Journey from the Minor Leagues to the World Series*. New York: Ballantine Books, 2008.

Feinstein, John. *Where Nobody Knows Your Name: Life in the Minor Leagues of Baseball*. New York: Anchor Books, 2015.

Kettmann, Steve. *Baseball Maverick: How Sandy Alderson Revolutionized Baseball and Revived the Mets*. New York: Atlantic Monthly Press, 2015.

Kvach, John F., Charity Ethridge, Michelle Hopkins, and Susanna Leberman. *Huntsville*. Charleston SC: Arcadia Publishing, 2013.

Larson, Greg. *Clubbie: A Minor League Baseball Memoir*. Lincoln: University of Nebraska Press, 2021.

Longenhagen, Eric. *Future Value: The Battle for Baseball's Soul and How Teams Will Find the Next Superstar*. Chicago: Triumph Books, 2021.

Marks, Henry S., and John Pruett. *The Huntsville Historical Review*. Vol. 9. Huntsville: Huntsville-Madison County Historical Society, 1979.

McCarter, Mark. *Never a Bad Game*. New York: Augustus Publications, 2020.

Neufeld, Michael. *Von Braun: Dreamer of Space, Engineer of War*. New York: Vintage Books, 2008.

Nipper, Skip. *Baseball in Nashville*. Charleston SC: Arcadia Publishing, 2007.

Peterson, Gary. *Battle of the Bay*. Chicago: Triumph Books, 2014.

Tafoya, Dale. *Bash Brothers: A Legacy Subpoenaed*. Dulles VA: Potomac Books, 2008.

————. *Billy Ball: Billy Martin and the Resurrection of the Oakland A's.* Guilford CT: Lyons Press, 2020.

Thomas, Gilbert W. *How Baseball Happened: Outrageous Lies Exposed! The True Story Revealed.* New York: David R. Godine Publishing, 2020.

Woody, Larry. *Schmittou: A Grand Slam in Baseball, Business, and Life.* Nashville: Eggman Publishing, 1996.

Index